SECRET PLACES

A Guide to 25 Little Known Scenic
Treasures of the New York's
Niagara-Allegany Region,
Including the Beautiful, the Bizarre, the
Spectacular and the Sublime.

By Bruce Kershner

Photographs by the author

KENDALL/HUNT PUBLISHING COMPANY
4050 Westmark Drive Dubuque, Iowa 52002

This author assumes no personal responsibility for any actions, or results
of these actions, of the reader in choosing to visit the features described
in this book.

SECRET PLACES
of the Niagara-Allegany Region

MAPS

SECRET PLACES
of the Niagara-Allegany Region
TABLE OF CONTENTS

Fig. 1. Secret Places Locator Map

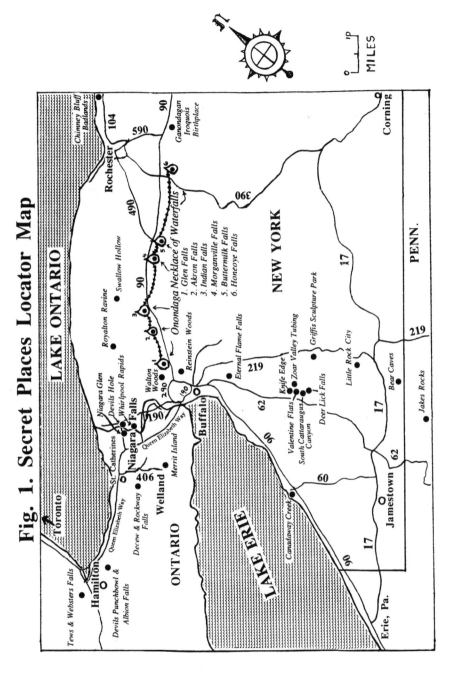

MILES

LAKE ONTARIO

Chimney Bluff Badlands

Rochester

104

90

590

490

90

Ganondagan Iroquois Birthplace

Swallow Hollow

Royalton Ravine

Onondaga Necklace of Waterfalls
1. Glen Falls
2. Akron Falls
3. Indian Falls
4. Morganville Falls
5. Buttermilk Falls
6. Honeoye Falls

390

NEW YORK

17

Griffis Sculpture Park

Little Rock City

219

Reinstein Woods

Eternal Flame Falls

219

Knife Edge

Zoar Valley Tubing

Bear Caves

Jakes Rocks

17

Deer Lick Falls

South Cattaraugus Canyon

Valentine Flats

62

90

Buffalo

290

Walton Woods

Merrit Island

Queen Elizabeth Way

190

Niagara Falls

St. Catherines

Niagara Glen

Devils Hole

Whirlpool Rapids

Welland

406

Decew & Rockway Falls

Queen Elizabeth Way

ONTARIO

Toronto

Hamilton

Tews & Websters Falls

Devils Punchbowl & Albion Falls

LAKE ERIE

Canadaway Creek

60

62

Jamestown

17

90

Erie, Pa.

PENN.

Corning

ii

Acknowledgements

A book like this takes at least two things: the freedom to roam and the freedom to write. I want to thank my dear wife, Helene, for giving me the opportunity to do both, and for giving me her unending patience, love and support. She also conceived of the idea for this book when all I had were files of maps and notes. I want to thank my children, Joshua and Libby, for accompanying me on some of my explorations. You may have made them a little slower, but you also made them, well ... a bit more "interesting."

I am in deep gratitude to my parents, Morris and Pearl, for encouraging me to become a naturalist, and also giving me the freedom to explore and learn about nature. You have enriched my life immeasurably.

Lastly, I want to thank Mother Nature and her Creator for giving us these treasures of nature at our doorstep and for making our world full of wonder, fascination and reverence.

About Bruce Kershner

Bruce Kershner is a well-known naturalist, ecologist and educator in Western New York. He earned his Bachelor of Science in biology from Binghamton University and his Master of Science in Plant Ecology from the University of Connecticut. He is a national authority on old growth forests, edible wild plants and waterfalls and has authored three books on these subjects. He currently is a science teacher at Cheektowaga-Sloan's JFK High School. Previously, he was senior environmentalist for Great Lakes United, an international coalition to clean up the Great Lakes. His honors include "Environmentalist of the Year" in 1987 and 1988 from Sierra Club (Niagara Group) and the Adirondack Mountain Club; two National Gold Medals for writing from the national Council for the Advancement & Support of Education; and "Best Children's TV Show in New York State" in 1991 by the N.Y. State Association of Broadcasters. He has served on the Erie County (NY) Environmental Management Council, the Town of Amherst (NY) Open Space Committee, the Nature Conservancy's Western NY Board of Governors and was manager of one of its preserves. He is active on many environmental issues with the Sierra Club, Nature Conservancy, Adirondack Mountain Club, Friends of Pine-Oak Woods (Staten Island, NY) and Friends of the ReinsteinWoods.

INTRODUCTION

The Niagara and Allegany Regions* possess a wealth of scenic spectacles and curiosities. However, few of the region's residents are aware of these, except for the most publicized sights, e.g. Niagara Falls, Letchworth Park.

This field guide presents some of these little known and seldom seen scenic treasures. **Most of these sights have never been described and mapped in detail in any publication, until now!** They are a privileged selection of 25 of the most notable scenic delights explored by the author in his ramblings over the landscape.

Where else can you find out where to see natural Eternal Flames, experience frog orgies, see a waterfall that turns on and off (on schedule), or observe a 100-foot high Ice Volcano! Or thrill at the largest waves on the continent, step back into time by entering a hushed Ancient Forest, marvel at the castles, spires and dragon's back of the Badlands, or get spiritual on the hill where the Iroquois nation was born!

The features described here are only a few of the region's more than 400 waterfalls, dozens of canyons and gorges, 60 caves and 29 "rock cities," as well as primeval forest remnants, nature preserves and parks. This guide is not meant to be complete, but just to introduce you to *some* of these "Secret Places," and to whet your appetite to experience more.

Some of these scenic delights are easy to get to and explore. Others, however, are not meant for the novice and the unseasoned. These other sights are challenging, strenuous and require safety precautions. Some of the unusual options offered include night hikes, off-trail walking, cave exploring, and climbing up very steep slopes. This book offers something for both the novice and the avid Nature lover, who want to see the very best that Nature has to offer.

*the region covered by this book covers the 12 westernmost counties of New York and Ontario's Niagara Peninsula. It stretches from the city of Hamilton, Ontario, in the west, across Buffalo and Niagara Falls, and east to the Rochester area. Southward, it extends to the Pennsylvania border from Allegany County to Chautauqua County (with Pennsylvania's Allegheny National Forest thrown in for good measure).

Some of the suggested outings take place on private land. Respect this fact, and enter the land quietly, without disturbing anything or leaving anything behind, and follow all safety precautions. Most landowners will appreciate this and will have no qualms about your presence.

Remember, the disrespectful, the litterers, the partiers and the reckless are the ones who anger landowners and ruin it for everyone else. Regarding safety, remember to use extreme caution near cliff edges, the edge of the Niagara River, while climbing up the sides of steep slopes, or while caving.

There are dozens more "Secret Places" in our region like the ones described here: the beautiful, the bizarre, the spectacular and the sublime. When you are done experiencing the ones in this book, I hope you will be eager to discover the others!

One last note about the "secret places" described in this book: "Once the secret's out, it's no longer a secret." The author fully acknowledges this dilemma. If more people know about them, there is the concern that their seclusion or pristineness could be diminished. On the other hand, without a core of people who have fallen in love with these special treasures, there is no constituency to watch out for and care about them. Some of our region's greatest natural wonders have been threatened by people more interested in profits and exploitation than in protecting Nature or the public's quality of life.

In recent years, there have been serious attempts to open Allegany State Park to large-scale logging and mining, to flood Letchworth State Park, and to dam up Zoar Valley. There is interest by the government in building a road into Valentine Flats to log its forest, and to build railroad tracks in the Niagara Gorge.

Many of our most beloved natural treasures were set aside for protection in spite of great opposition from those who had other designs for them. Niagara Falls itself is the earliest such example.

Remember that the job of caring about and fighting to protect these wonders ultimately falls upon the people who know and care about them. That is one additional reason for "letting the secret out" about these places.

These natural sights are there for you to enjoy. May your lives be enriched by the experience.

THE ANCIENT FORESTS OF REINSTEIN WOODS

Without question, the most beautiful natural sight in the entire Buffalo metropolitan area -- and the next place you should visit if you haven't seen it! It is the only place you can see the original landscape just as it looked before the Indians encountered Europeans. It is a fascinating landscape of virgin forest and huge trees, brilliant autumn foliage, dozens of secluded ponds and wetlands, easy-to-see wildlife, historic carvings dating back to the mid-1800s.

Distance: The guided walk is two miles long.

Level of Difficulty: Easy

Notable Features:

Dr. Reinstein and The Nature Preserve: The 280-acre preserve was the former estate of Dr. Victor Reinstein. He was a physician, attorney and real estate tycoon, and one of our area's greatest public benefactors. He also appreciated natural beauty -- and recognized a scenic gem when he encountered it in his real estate purchases. After acquiring much of then-undeveloped southern Cheektowaga, he selected this stand of ancient forest and wetland to become his private preserve. In the 1930s and 1940s, he created two dozen ponds for wildlife, and laid out an extensive system of woods trails. Shortly after he purchased the site, he envisioned donating it to the public at a later time to protect it in perpetuity. He did that in his will and the estate became the Reinstein Woods State Nature Preserve in 1986. At that time, it also came under the protection of the New York State Constitution and its "Forever Wild" clause. With the generosity of Mrs. Julia Reinstein, his widow, the Preserve was expanded again in 1991.

For those who want to learn more about the natural and human history of the preserve, read *Buffalo's Backyard Wilderness: An Ecological Study of the Reinstein Woods State Nature Preserve*, by Bruce Kershner (Canisius College Press & Western NY Heritage Institute, 2001 Main St., Buffalo, NY 14208, (716) 888-2706). It is also available in area libraries.

The Ancient Forest: What is astonishing is that the preserve contains what may be **the most valuable piece of natural real**

Tree hugging welcome! This ancient yellow birch is near record size.

estate in Erie County -- an 80-acre ancient forest that looks much like it did in prehistoric times. Numerous cherry, sugar maple and beech trees up to five-feet in diameter are set in a pristine forest primeval scene. Some have been measured at more than 200 years old. Some beech trees have carved initials of early settlers carvings dating back to Civil War time. **It is one of the largest virgin forests in New York State and one of the only old growth forests to be located in the middle of any metropolitan area in the U.S.** Also found here is a rare wildflower, the winged monkeyflower, discovered in 1990, that was last seen in western New York in 1864! The forest's autumn color spectacle is fantastic, in fact the best in the Buffalo metropolitan area.

The Ponds: Two dozen lakes, ponds and marshes are scattered throughout the preserve. What is striking about one of the largest ponds is that it is covered by "shocking pink" water lilies that create a photographer's and painter's dream. In fact, Lily Pond reminds many of the famous Monet painting of water lilies. In essence, the Preserve is a living "million-dollar painting" and raises the question, "Does art imitate nature, or does nature imitate art?"

The Wildlife: The preserve is one of the best places to easily see wildlife in western New York. Four-foot high great blue herons, coyote, beaver (and beaver dams and dens), deer, mink, snapping and painted turtles, pileated woodpeckers, Canada geese, wood ducks and many other wildlife species are often observable.

The Historical Heritage: The Preserve is one of the few places where history buffs have as much to appreciate as do nature buffs and lovers of beauty. The Ancient Forest represents a unique and under-appreciated historic treasure: a view of what the original landscape looked like before white settlers cut it all down and modified it forever. Today, it looks like it did when it was the Indian hunting ground. In addition, almost 75 trees have historic carvings, some dating back to the 1800s, including the initials of early settlers, as well as those of the common folk and lovers in every decade since. (Of course, carving on these trees today is illegal and vandalistic. At what point graffiti becomes historic carvings is an interesting point to ponder.) There are also markers still visible from the original Holland Land Survey of 1797.

The preserve can only be visited on most Wednesday or Saturday mornings in spring, summer and autumn. Organized groups can arrange a tour for any time by calling for a reservation. A

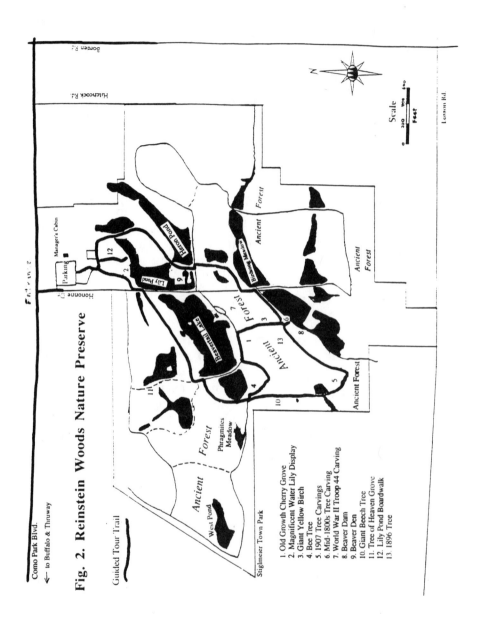

Fig. 2. Reinstein Woods Nature Preserve

Guided Tour Trail

1. Old Growth Cherry Grove
2. Magnificent Water Lily Display
3. Giant Yellow Birch
4. Bee Tree
5. 1907 Tree Carvings
6. Mid-1800s Tree Carving
7. World War II Troop 44 Carving
8. Beaver Dam
9. Beaver Den
10. Giant Beech Tree
11. Tree of Heaven Grove
12. Lily Pond Boardwalk
13. 1896 Tree

rewarding guided tour is provided. Visitors are not allowed to roam the Preserve on their own. For information on the exact hours of the tours, call (716) 683-5959.

The tour takes two or so hours. Bring camera, binoculars and identification guides. *In summer, mosquito repellant is a must!*

Directions:

From Ontario, cross into Buffalo via the Peace Bridge and take Rt. 190 south to the NY Thruway (Rt. 90) and take the Thruway East. From points south and west of Buffalo, also take Thruway East. From Rochester and points east, take the Thruway West. The Thruway will take you to Exit 52 east (Walden Avenue) From Buffalo, take Walden Avenue east toward Cheektowaga.

Exit the Thruway at Exit 52 east, and take Walden Avenue to Union Road (Rt. 277). Turn right (south) onto Union Road. Continue past the railroad overpasses until Como Park Blvd. Turn left (east) onto Como Park Blvd. After about 1.5 miles, look for the wooden Reinstein Preserve sign on your right. Turn right on Honorine Drive to the entrance. Once in the Preserve, the trail guide will take you on a delightful tour.

Magnificent waterlily display on Lily Pond.

ETERNAL FLAME FALLS

Keep this hike a secret! It is too special to give away to people who might abuse it with litter or vandalism. It is a challenging but short hike to the bottom of a 35-foot waterfall and secluded gorge which has a feature that is truly unique: **one to three natural flames that flare from inside a grotto that is washed over by part of a waterfall!**

Distance: 1.5 mile round trip

Level of Difficulty: Moderate in daylight, difficult at night. First half of walk is on a wide trail; last half is off-trail walking down a slope and then along a brook bed. Wear proper footwear for getting a little wet or muddy. Night hike requires flashlights.

Features:

Shale Creek Preserve: Isolated southern part of Chestnut Ridge County Park, open to walking and nature study only. This portion has many trails through cool hemlock, maple and pine forest.

Shale Creek Gorge :   150-foot deep ravine which contains the Eternal Flame and Eternal Flame Falls.

Eternal Flame Falls: A 35-foot waterfall that leaps over two steps and cascades over layered shale in an exquisitely scenic and graceful manner. A small portion of it drapes over the Eternal Flame's little grotto.

The Eternal Flame: Natural gas jets, 3 to 9" long (depending on natural pressure changes) that flare out of the base of the waterfall. At night, they appear as an eerie flickering light from the top of the gorge, and as a ghostly "campfire" from the bottom of the gorge, at a distance. It is a mystical and memorable sight. **It may in fact be the only occurrence in the world of a natural flame that lies under and behind a waterfall!**

The gas pressure varies and the flame occasionally goes out. If you arrive and there is no flame, take a cigarette lighter and flick it along the bottom edge of the back wall of the three-foot wide grotto at the lower right base of the waterfall (see illustration). You will notice little bubbles coming up through a crack on the edge of a puddle in the grotto. Don't worry, the flame does not "blow up" and will not set you on fire -- it is a very tame flame. However, you should be careful on your approach to the grotto. The rocks are slippery.

During the winter, ice flow formations and spring time flooding also put the flame out. It is lit by visitors each spring.

Note: Because of the unusual "Eternal Flame," it is most impressive when seen in the dark. The best way for the first-time visitor is to visit it in the day and memorize the off-trail route. Then visit it a second time in very late afternoon, 30 minutes before sunset, so that you walk down to it in the light but arrive at the flame in twilight. Remember to take flashlights.

While you marvel at Eternal Flame, the white noise of the waterfall and the mysteriousness of the night forest will result in an experience you will never forget! Some visitors feel a spiritual reverence in this remarkable spot.

Important: **Bring plastic bags** with you so you can clean up the environment! When you leave, carry out bottles and litter that other less caring souls leave, so that this special place can remain special.

Directions:

From Ontario, take the Queen Elizabeth Way to the Peace Bridge and then onto Rt. 190 South to the NY Thruway (Rt. 90) west. From Buffalo, Rochester and points east, take the NY Thruway west. From the south, take Rt. 219 north or the NY Thruway east. For those taking the Thruway, exit the Thruway onto Rt. 219 south (a four-lane divided highway at this point).

From Rt. 219, take Armor Duells Rd. exit. Turn east onto Armor Duells Road. One half mile later, you will come to Rt. 277 (Chestnut Ridge Rd.); turn right (south). Pass the main entrance of Chestnut Ridge Park as you ascend a long hill. Shortly after you pass Gartman Road on the left, bear right around a wide curve. Shortly after the curve, take the first right onto Seyfert Rd. Only 100 yards along Seyfert, park along the road next to a gated dirt road entrance on the right. This is the Shale Creek Preserve entrance. Enter this gated road on foot.

Follow the pretty woods road into an open field. Hug the right side of the field, and re-enter the woods on a trail. Do not cross the middle of the field or you will get off course.

Now a woods trail, it curves and descends a steep hill to a brook crossing. This is Shale Creek. After crossing the brook, the main trail turns sharply left and uphill. It enters a dark hemlock and pine forest and the trail, while wide, becomes less clear among the straight rows of pines. Always bear left (toward the edge of the ravine), rather than taking rightward trails. After a 100 or so yards, the trail will take you to the edge of the gorge. Where the sound of rushing water is loudest, you can look down into the 150-foot deep gorge where the falls and flame are. In the daylight from the top of the cliff, the flame is undetectable; at night, it will be a distant orange glow down in the black abyss below you. **Take caution at the edge -- it is a lethal drop if you slip!**

Follow the trail *along the edge of the ravine* and it will descend steeply downhill. When you reach the bottom of the hill, peer through the woods and you will notice a stream in a shallow ravine to your left. Cut left off the trail through the woods to the secluded brook.

Follow the brook all the way upstream, until you reach the falls and flame. You'll be jumping rocks, scurrying over fallen logs and branches -- this is a *wild* stream. Either wear hiking boots or sneakers that can get wet or muddy. Some people elect to walk in the brook itself.

After standing in amazement at the flame and falls, you can return the same way you came. But for the even more adventurous, the short way home is by climbing up the right margin of the falls, when the flow of the waterfall is low in summer. Use the strategically placed tree roots and rock corners as safe hand-holds. With step-by-step maneuvers, this route takes you to the upper level. It is easier than it looks, and you should not get wet. **Remember, this route is only for more experienced hikers.** Once at the top level, walk through or along the stream until you intersect with the woods trail crossing. Turn right onto the trail and return to your car.

Eternal Flame at the bottom of Eternal Flame Falls

Fig. 3.
Eternal Flame Falls

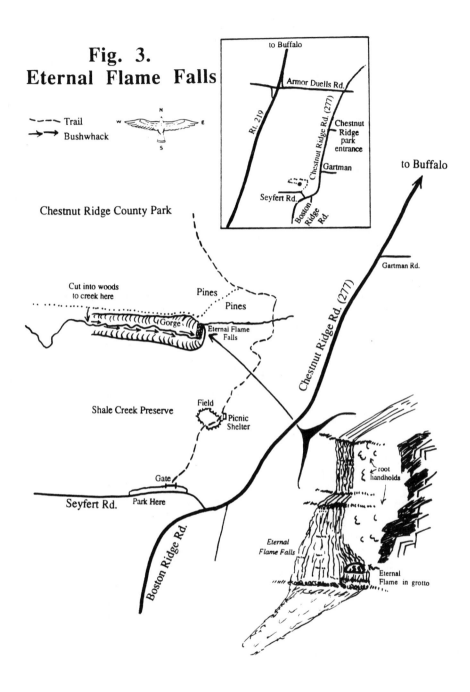

Trail ----
Bushwhack →

N
W   E
S

to Buffalo
Armor Duells Rd.
Rt. 219
Chestnut Ridge Rd. (277)
Chestnut Ridge park entrance
Gartman
Seyfert Rd.
Boston Ridge Rd.

Chestnut Ridge County Park

to Buffalo

Gartman Rd.

Cut into woods to creek here

Pines
Pines

Gorge

Eternal Flame Falls

Chestnut Ridge Rd. (277)

Shale Creek Preserve

Field

Picnic Shelter

Gate

Seyfert Rd.   Park Here

Boston Ridge Rd.

root handholds

Eternal Flame Falls

Eternal Flame in grotto

WEAVING YOUR WAY THROUGH WALTON WOODS

Peaceful walk or bike through a little-known forested park with natural and paved trails that loop around scenic lakes. Its location in Amherst, a short walk from SUNY Buffalo's campus, makes it a surprise to many area residents.

Distance: Trail system loops total seven miles.

Level of Difficulty: Easy

Notable Features:

Walton Woods: A 52-acre Town of Amherst Park that is known by few citizens outside the Audubon New Community. It contains two lakes, bike and nature trails that wind through forest, around the lakes, and around the periphery of the residential area.

One of its surprises is a 6-acre **old growth forest**, an extremely rare feature in Western New York. The old growth or "virgin" forest contains 150-year old, four-foot diameter beech and tulip trees with very beautiful spring wildflowers.

Another surprise are several vest-pocket playgrounds, hidden in the deep woods. After walking or bicycling on the trails, they provide a perfect break for a family. After the kids get their thrills on the tire swings, climbing equipment and slides, you can hop back on the trail and be on your way again!

A visit to Walton Woods offers an excellent:

1) scenic, contemplative walk

2) leisurely bike ride. It connects up easily with the five-mile long Ellicott Creek Bikeway that runs from North Forest Road (just north of Maple Road) and ends at Niagara Falls Blvd. The Walton Woods bikeway and the Ellicott Creek bikeway are connected by Audubon Parkway.

4) local cross country ski

3) superb night hike. In April and early May, the spring peeper frog chorus makes a weirdly enjoyable night walk. In summer, hooting owls and the katydid cacophony are an evening treat. Although the park officially closes at night, it is used regularly by local residents for evening walks and jogs.

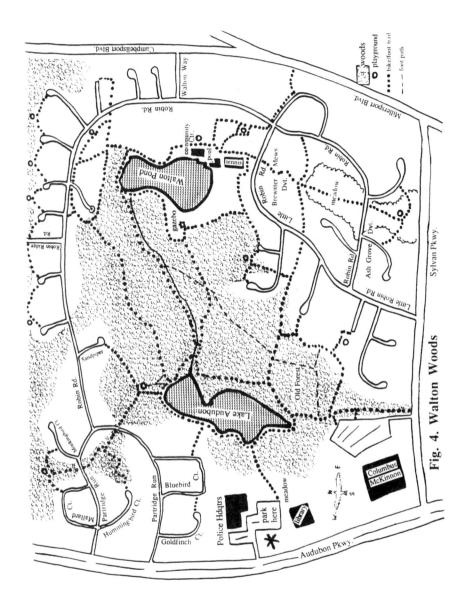

Fig. 4. Walton Woods

Directions:

From Buffalo, take Rt. 290 to the Rt. 263 North (Millersport Highway) exit. From Ontario, take the Queenston-Lewiston Bridge into the U.S. and travel south on Rt. 190, crossing Grand Island to Rt. 290 east. From points south or east of Buffalo, take the NY Thruway to Exit 50 (Rt. 290).

From the Rt. 263 north exit of Rt. 290, take Millersport Road (Rt. 263) north, past SUNY Buffalo campus to North Forest Road. Turn left onto North Forest Road. In 1/2 mile is Audubon Parkway. Turn right (north). About 3/4 mile later, turn right into the driveway for the Town of Amherst Police Department headquarters. Pull your car into the parking lot that is furthest to the right and park at the end where the trail begins.

Once on the paved trail, you will shortly come to secluded Lake Audubon. If you turn right, you will head toward the old growth forest stand. After the trail leaves the lake, you will come to a fork in the paved trail; take the right fork. Two hundred feet later is an *unpaved* foot trail into the woods on your left (just before a another fork in the paved trail). Take the foot path and you will pass through the old forest. As you walk, notice the large beech and tulip trees to your left. Trillium are abundant in the spring. If you head left *off* the trail into the grove, you can find a "widow maker," named by loggers (who fortunately never got to this stand!) because of what happens to a wife when such a large hanging branch falls on her husband. The widow maker is the upper half of a tree trunk suspended 30 feet up. The tree broke in a storm many year ago; the lower part fell to the ground, the upper part got stuck in the trunk of another tree.

The dirt trail will cross the paved trail a short while later. Take a left here and it will take you to Lake Audubon (on the other side is where your car is parked). If you want to continue on the nature trail, turn right, walk 75 feet, and turn left onto the dirt trail. The trail has a muddy section in spring and after rainy periods. The nature trail crosses two paved trails, and ends at a third paved trail.

Whether on foot or on bike, reward your spirit of exploration and wander along all the peaceful trails that loop their way around the park. Just follow as many trails as you wish. The trail system seems confusing, but sooner or later, you end up back at Lake Audubon where you can return to your car. You can consult the map if needed.

The trails will loop every which way through woods, around ponds, along quiet residential areas and into cul-de-sacs and past hidden playgrounds. One loop takes you along willow-lined Walton Pond along the margin of the woods, including a picturesque circular bandstand shelter. This is a perfect place for lunch or shelter from rain. If you're bike riding, you will cover all the trails within 90 minutes.

If you want to hook up with the Amherst Bikeway that parallels Ellicott Creek, drive your bike to the parking lot and turn left on Audubon Parkway. Less than a mile later, you'll cross North Forest Road and a bridge over Ellicott Creek. You can get onto the bikeway to your left just after the creek. The bikeway goes two miles one direction, three miles the other.

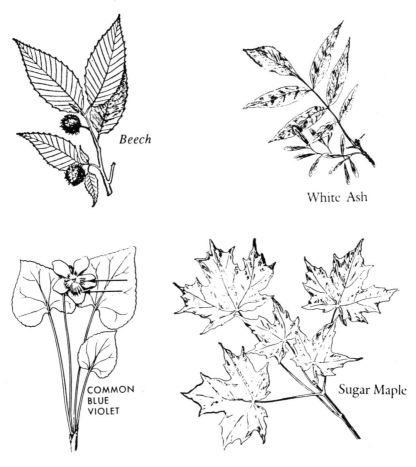

Beech

White Ash

COMMON
BLUE
VIOLET

Sugar Maple

WHIRLPOOL RAPIDS TREK

One of the most exciting hikes in the eastern U.S., **past the largest series of standing waves in North America**!

Distance: 3 miles or 5 miles, depending upon choice of route.

Difficulty: Difficult and challenging. For experienced hikers only along the trailless stretch. Trailed route is moderate to easy.

Notable Features:

Niagara Gorge: Descend into the wild Niagara Gorge, including the wildest portion called the "Impassable Zone." Despite the world popularity of Niagara Falls, and the presence of the twin cities of Niagara Falls on both sides of the Niagara Gorge, the Whirlpool Rapids stretch is truly wild and challenging to hike and contains spectacular scenery. The 7-mile long gorge is 250 feet deep at this point, with overhanging chalky cliffs.

Whirlpool Rapids: A world-class phenomena. They are the largest series of standing waves of any whitewater in North America, and among the most dangerous rapids as well. Standing Great Waves reach 12 to 18 feet high, curl under themselves, crash, shift and churn with awesome power. Some liken them to tsunamis ("tidal waves"). There are 8 to 10 of these Great Waves in succession. Unlike most whitewater, the river is very deep here, 40-feet deep. Hence the waves are not caused by the force of swift-moving water over shallow boulders. Instead, they are caused by the huge volume of water flowing out of the world's greatest lake system, and being forced through a narrow channel. A less violent section of the river, called the Eddy Basin, ends with one giant, always-curling, green wave just before you reach the Whirlpool Basin.

Seeing the violence, size and intimidating motion of these waves leaves most visitors remarking that the experience is riveting. Some feel the vibration in their bodies, especially when lying on a boulder near the river edge.

The Impassable Zone: This section of the gorge was covered by a landslide decades ago. The rock fall blocked the wide trail that used to traverse it, leading to its being called "impassable." Despite the intimidating label, there is now a thin thread of a trail along the upper end of the gravel slope that has formed along the

One of the Great Waves of the Whirlpool Rapids

bottom edge of the cliff face. Being 100 feet higher than the raging river, the vista it provides over the torrential scene is almost as memorable as seeing the Great Waves from the shoreline.

Titan Rock. A colossal (40 feet high) boulder that fell long ago from the top of the Niagara Escarpment and stopped at the edge of the raging river, slightly overhanging it.

Maid-of-the-Mist Pool: The trail passes above this green, swirling pool created by Niagara Falls, when it was carving its way up the canyon thousands of years ago. The pool averages 180 to 200 feet deep, a great depth for an inland river. From the trail above, the pool's surface seems relatively smooth, but is actually very rough due to violent boiling up of water currents called upwelling.

Whirlpool Bridge: The trail passes under this double bridge span, just before the "Impassable Zone" is reached. The bridge collapsed in the early part of this century due to ice blocks that formed in the river. The remains of the bridge can be seen along the shore of the river directly below the current bridge.

Whirlpool Basin: See description under Devils Hole Hike.

Caution: This hike requires care along the entire route of cliffs, boulders, and slick river-edge rock surfaces. Remember, one slip into the violent Niagara River Rapids is lethal. Stay clear of the edge!

Directions:

From points south and west of Buffalo, take the NY Thruway (Rt. 90 east) to exit 53 and follow Rt. 190 north. From Rochester and points east, take the NY Thruway west to Rt. 290 (Exit 50) which ends at Rt. 190 north. Once on Rt. 190, take it north from Buffalo across Grand Island and then exit onto the Robert Moses Parkway. From Ontario, take the Queen Elizabeth Way to Rt. 420 to Niagara Falls and cross the Rainbow Bridge into the U.S.

Now in downtown Niagara Falls, follow signs to the Niagara Aquarium and park in their lot. Cross the street next to the Aquarium and walk *toward* the gorge and the parkway, and you will encounter a small road that parallels the parkway, only 75 feet from the Aquarium. Turn right onto this road, heading north, away from the Rainbow Bridge direction. This quiet road will pass under the parkway through a short tunnel. Once through the tunnel, stay to the left side of the road. When you come upon several piles of dirt, that is where the Niagara Gorge access trail begins. The gorge edge is just 30 feet to your left. Take this slightly hidden dirt road down into the gorge. It will hug the edge of the cliff as it descends.

When it enters a wooded, natural stretch, there will be two places where you can look upstream across the sea-green **Maid-of-the-Mist Pool** and see Niagara Falls beautifully framed by the Rainbow Bridge. There are also places where you can hear the roar of both Niagara Falls *and* the roar of the Whirlpool Rapids (in separate ears). At other places, you can only hear the roar of the rapids or the roar of Niagara Falls, but not both! See if you can find each of these spots. Cupping each ear with your hands will assist you.

Take the trail until it passes under the **Whirlpool Rapids Bridge**. You will see the bridge abutments and girders coming out of the now-impressive cliff. The trail will become more exciting as you skirt deeply eroded areas of trail, and as the river's roar heightens.

Right after this point, you enter the "**Impassable Zone.**" The trail turns right and uphill through an open wooded steep slope. It gets more and more steep, obscure and narrow. When the lightly wooded section ends, you enter the scree slope, the gravel embankment that skirts the bottom of the cliff. It looks intimidating, but is not dangerous if you take care to stay on the upper part of the gravel slope, not the cliff edge below. Follow the thin thread of trail as it ascends the scree slope. It then stays rather level for a ways, following the bottom of the upper cliff. Stop to enjoy the spectacular gorge and **Whirlpool Rapids** spectacle before you.

During this stretch, the part of the river directly below you will be obscured by a line of shrubs that also hides a 30-foot ledge. Soon you will come to a stretch with a clear view all the way down to the river to your left. After you pass above that smooth gravel stretch, you will reach a rockier, scrubbier steep slope below you. Here is where you descend to the river. There is no choice but to slide down the slope on your butt. You will reach the very rocky but relatively flat corridor along the river edge. (While descending, if you come to any cliff higher than four feet, you have descended down the wrong part of the slope. Do not try to descend further, but go back up the slope and continue along it until you reach the correct part of the slope.) When you have finally gotten to the bottom, *look back and remember exactly where you came down* if you plan to return on the same route.

Weave your way downstream between the boulder jumbles, sometimes away from the river, sometimes right along the river.

Fig. 5. Whirlpool Rapids Trek

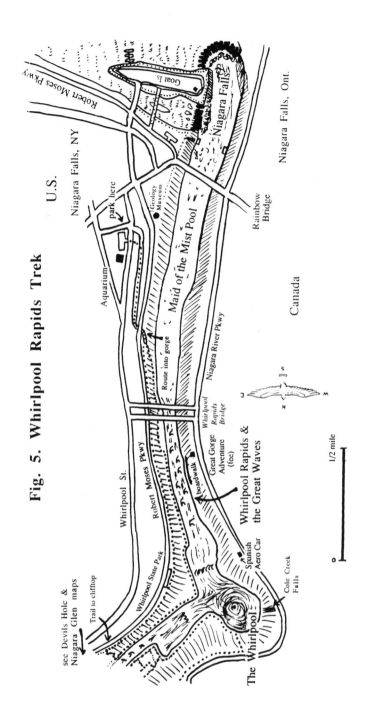

U.S.

Robert Moses Pkwy

Niagara Falls, NY

Goat Is.

Niagara Falls

Niagara Falls, Ont.

park here

Aquarium

Geology Museum

Maid of the Mist Pool

Rainbow Bridge

Canada

Route into gorge

Niagara River Pkwy

Whirlpool St.

Robert Moses Pkwy

Whirlpool Rapids Bridge

Great Gorge Adventure (fee)

boardwalk

Whirlpool Rapids & the Great Waves

1/2 mile

Whirlpool State Park

Spanish Aero Car

Cole Creek Falls

see Devils Hole & Niagara Glen maps

Trail to clifftop

The Whirlpool

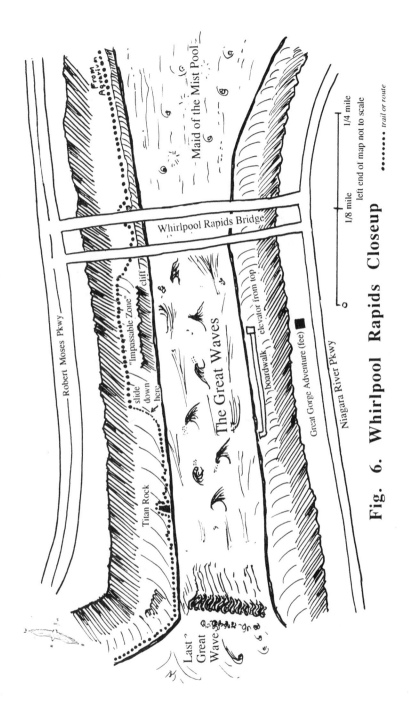

Fig. 6. Whirlpool Rapids Closeup

From Aquarium

Maid of the Mist Pool

Whirlpool Rapids Bridge

Robert Moses Pkwy

"Impassable Zone"

cliff

slide down here

The Great Waves

Titan Rock

boardwalk

elevator from top

Great Gorge Adventure (fee)

Niagara River Pkwy

Last Great Wave

1/4 mile

1/8 mile

0

left end of map not to scale

•••••• trail or route

Stop and marvel at the **Great Waves**. See how they stay in place, shifting here and there, lessening, then rising up and even falling backward upon themselves in a powerful display of spray and foam.

Remember that the river's water level changes often, leaving stretches of flat rock exposed and covered with extremely slick algae. Sometimes, surges of water suddenly cover these slick rocks. It is recommended to stay off any still-wet or slick and slimy rock terraces.

You will come to a 40-foot high boulder, **Titan Rock**, perched right on the edge of the raging river. On the downstream side of the boulder is a perfect lunch spot and place to feel the vibration of the river in your body. You can also climb under one of the boulders into a crevice that leads to the other boulder closer to the river. Look for this route!

At this point, you have two options. You can return the same way you came (1.5-mile trip back). Or you can continue on downstream to see the last Great Wave and the Whirlpool (2.5 mile trip back).

If you choose the longer return route, continue weaving your way downstream. Stop to marvel at the last Great Wave. Stand in awe at its green, curling majesty. As you continue on, the river and the cliff face will then turn to the right and you will pick up a formal trail again.

Observe the **Whirlpool** Basin, with its slowly spinning currents and eddies. This is where the great river takes a right-angle turn. The currents may not look it, but they are violent! People have seen 50-gallon metal drums suddenly thrust out of the water 20 feet. Apparently, these currents kept the drum submerged all the way from Niagara Falls (which it must have plunged over), then finally released it from the deeps of the river. Look across it to a waterfall **(Cole Creek Falls)** on the Canadian cliff face. This falls is 230 feet high, 50 feet higher than Niagara Falls, and the tallest in Ontario! Its flow is visible from a distance only in spring, early summer and after rainy periods.

Follow the river edge trail downstream and you will come to stone steps. Take them up the cliff face to civilization above. At the top, which is Whirlpool State Park, turn right and walk back home, walking between the gorge edge and the parkway as long as possible. **Note:** You can also combine this trek with the Devils Hole Hike for an all-day adventure.

DEVILS HOLE AND THE GREAT WHIRLPOOL

An exciting hike into the dramatic lower Niagara Gorge to Devil's Hole Cave near where an Indian massacre occurred long ago, past one of the Great Waves, other impressive rapids, and three other caves.

Distance: 4.5 to 5 miles

Difficulty: Moderate to easy at the bottom of the gorge, steep on the ascent up the stone steps.

Notable Features:

Niagara Gorge: This portion of the Niagara Gorge was carved by the ancient Niagara Falls 7000 to 8000 years ago. The Niagara Gorge is up to 315 feet deep and is **one of the most rugged gorges in eastern North America.** This is especially interesting since it is between the downtowns of the twin cities of Niagara Falls, NY and Niagara Falls, Ontario.

Devil's Hole Cave: A historically famous wide-mouth limestone cave near the bottom of the gorge. Its entrance is eight feet high and the cave is 50 feet long. The Devil's Hole Cave got its name because of the legend that it was associated with an evil curse bestowed by an Indian guide on the French explorer Sieur De La Salle. His expeditions were later accompanied by major mishaps, followed by his murder in 1687.

If you enter the cave, you do so at your own risk, since a rock fell off the cliff near the cave entrance in recent years. Because of this, the Parks Department discourages people from visiting the cave. Many people assumed the evil curse had already expired, but maybe the Parks Department knows better!

Devil's Hole Rapids: A series of churning four- to seven-foot high rapids in the Niagara River.

Devil's Hole Gulch: Steep ravine indented in the Gorge wall. Site of infamous 1763 massacre of British soldiers by Seneca warriors. A wagon train of 24 men was ambushed by a party of Senecas, angry at the fact that they had lost the business of portaging supplies around Niagara Falls. Only three men escaped. British soldiers rushed to the site, but the warriors massacred 90 more men!

Rock of Ages: Giant vertical 30-foot high boulder perched on the river edge.

Rock of Ages Cave: A 30-foot long, small cave found in the boulder jumble at the base of Rock of Ages. The entrance is a two-foot diameter "crawl-into" hole. It is located on the downstream (northeast) end of Rock of Ages, 4 feet below where a rough trail cuts off from the main trail to take you to the other side of the rock and to the river edge. Once inside, a passage to the right connects to a room. A passage to the left exits through another opening.

Driftwood Cave: This boulder cave is almost 80 feet long and is the crawl-on-your-knees kind. It is unique in that its ceiling is formed by a single 50-foot boulder. The cave has three entrances. The main one is 20 feet wide and two to three feet high. Driftwood is found inside the cave, brought there when the Niagara River used to submerge it. To locate it, walk roughly 100 or so steps downstream along the trail that you just walked (310 feet northeast of Rock of Ages Cave, to be precise).

Talus Cave: This 35-foot cave has an entrance 3 feet high and 9 feet wide, with a passage averaging three-feet high. To locate it, walk roughly 320 steps downstream along the trail away from Driftwood Cave.

The Whirlpool. Large round basin where the Niagara River takes a right-angle turn. Dangerous whirling currents carry floating objects 'round and 'round -- and sometimes suck them underwater, or shoot them out of the water. Despite its power, the Whirlpool is nothing like it was before the hydroelectric diversion reduced the river's water flow.

Cole Creek Cascade: A 230-foot waterfall that plunges down the Canadian escarpment above the Whirlpool. It is 50 feet higher than Niagara Falls (though nowhere as large). **It is the tallest waterfall in Ontario!**

Niagara Glen: See description under Niagara Glen Hike

The Great Wave and   See description under
   Whirlpool Rapids   Whirlpool Rapids Trek

Note: Bring a flashlight and compass if you want to locate and explore the caves described above.

Caution: Along the river, take care not to slip on the rocks or you will end up in treacherous currents!
You can combine this hike with the Whirlpool Rapids Trek to create an all-day challenging adventure.

Directions:

From points south of Buffalo, take the NY Thruway (Rt. 90) east to Rt. 190 north to Niagara Falls. From Rochester and points east of Buffalo, take NY Thruway west to Rt. 290 west, then Rt. 190 north to Niagara Falls. From Buffalo, take Rt. 190 north.

Once on Rt. 190 North, take it across Grand Island. At the end of the second bridge leaving Grand Island, exit onto Robert Moses Parkway to Niagara Falls downtown. The parkway ends at the Niagara Reservation and you exit onto local streets that veer you to the right. Drive several blocks till you see signs for the second section of the Robert Moses Parkway north. Turn left onto it and drive on the northbound lane until the exit for Devil's Hole State Park. Take pedestrian bridge across the parkway to the park.

From Ontario, take Queen Elizabeth Way to Niagara Falls and the Rainbow Bridge border crossing into the U.S. Drive several blocks till you see signs for the Robert Moses Parkway north. Follow directions as given in the previous paragraph.

Once in the park, go to the edge of the cliff and walk a short distance downstream to the Ongiara Trail entrance at a break in the cliff edge. Descend down the long flight of stone stairs and count the steps as you go. After 88 steps, a side trail to the right leads to the **Devil's Hole Cave**. However, it is blocked by a rock wall to obscure it and discourage people from using it because of the Parks Department's fears about falling rocks near the cave.

From where the main trail meets the Devils Hole side trail, it continues down to the bottom of the gorge. Once at the bottom of the trail, turn left upstream. You will pass along the bottom of **Devil's Hole Gulch** (can you sense the spirits?). A half-mile later, you'll reach the striking **Rock of Ages**, a mammoth boulder that once was part of the cliff face directly above you. Look for its cave (see above description). To find **Driftwood** and **Talus Caves**, follow the directions given above.

Note the imposing 280-foot cliffs above you. Admire the violent **Devil's Hole Rapids** and swift currents in front of you. **Remember that the entire drainage of the world's greatest lake system is flowing through this narrow point before your eyes!** On the opposite shore is Canada and the beautiful Niagara Glen (see separate entry).

A quarter-mile after Rock of Ages, you will come to picnic tables and the bottom of the trail that takes you back up to the road. The Ongiara Trail continues ahead.

You may choose to return to your car here or walk an additional one mile to see the impressive last Great Wave of the Whirlpool Rapids and the Whirlpool Basin. If you choose to return, walk up the Great Stone Staircase (340 steps, count'em!). Shortly after you start walking up, notice a boulder cave on your right formed by two massive boulders. About 125 steps from the bottom is another rock shelter under a boulder to the left. Once at the top, turn left, and walk between the cliff edge and the parkway for 0.9 mile until you reach the pedestrian bridge to your car.

If you chose the second option, follow the trail upstream. The trail will get rougher and narrower as it approaches the last Great Wave, a green, violent, curling, chillingly powerful wave at the upstream edge of the Whirlpool. The wave is part of the **Whirlpool Rapids, the largest standing waves in North America!** Observe the Whirlpool and its curling eddies, rip currents and upwellings. The flow may look gentle, but it's Lethal. Look to the opposite shore to see 230-foot Cole Creek Falls, visible only in spring (see description under Niagara Glen).

After you've seen these sights, go down stream to the Great Stone Stairs and follow the directions given above.

Devil' s Hole Cave

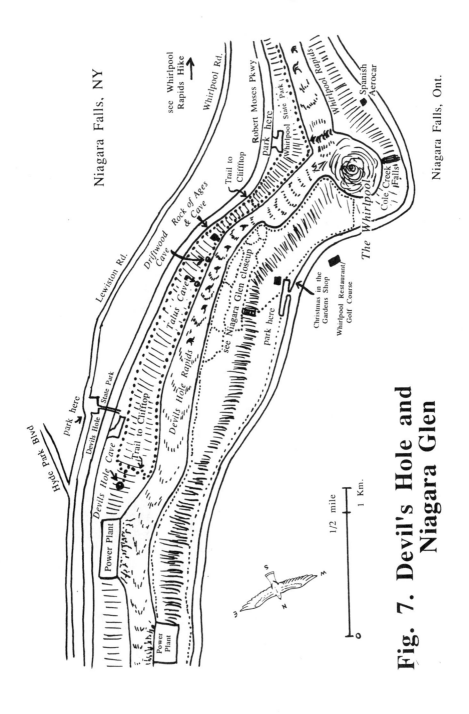

Fig. 7. Devil's Hole and Niagara Glen

Niagara Falls, NY

Niagara Falls, Ont.

see Whirlpool Rapids Hike

Whirlpool Rd.

Robert Moses Pkwy

Park here

Whirlpool State Park

Whirlpool Rapids

Spanish Aerocar

Trail to Clifftop

Driftwood Cave

Rock of Ages & Cave

Lewiston Rd.

Talus Cave

The Whirlpool

Cole Creek Falls

see Niagara Glen closeup

park here

Devils Hole Rapids

Christmas in the Gardens Shop

Whirlpool Restaurant/ Golf Course

Hyde Park Blvd

Park here

State Park

Devils Hole Cave

Trail to Clifftop

Power Plant

Power Plant

1/2 mile

1 Km.

0

S

E

W

N

NIAGARA GLEN AND ITS WEIRD
ROCK FORMATIONS

A fascinating walk through the Niagara Glen, an unusual, boulder-strewn terrace perched above the mighty Niagara River, with giant potholes, colossal boulders, rock formations, rock shelters, vistas, rare plants and high cliffs. The churning Devil's Hole Rapids add an additional excitement.

Distance: 1.8 miles/3 kilometers

Difficulty: Easy to moderate, varying with rockiness of terrain.

Notable Features:

Niagara Glen: A rocky terrace below the Niagara Escarpment (a line of cliffs) and above the rushing Niagara River. The terrace was carved out when the ancient Niagara Falls was grinding its way through this part of the gorge, perhaps 6000 years ago. Colossal boulders cracked off from the top of the overhanging cliffs over the millennia, landing on the Glen in a scattered jumble and creating a weird and scenic forest setting. The moist, undisturbed habitat of the Glen allows rare wildflowers to grow.

Niagara Escarpment: The 150-foot high line of overhanging cliffs above the Glen and the Niagara River. See detailed description of this under Tews Falls entry. A special, free-standing, caged-in staircase takes the visitor from the roadside area above to the Glen below. The staircase itself is an exciting experience.

Rock Formations: Numerous odd rock formations can be seen in the Glen. Examples are:

> *Devil's Oven Pot Hole* - A five-foot wide, natural, vertical hole or chimney carved by the roaring ancient Niagara Falls. This and the following pot holes were created by violent churning of water under the ancient Niagara Falls when it was carving its way through this part of the gorge perhaps 6000 years ago.
>
> *Twin Pot Holes* - Two more large, vertical holes in giant boulders that suggest staring eyes.
>
> *Fat Man's Misery Pot Hole* - a smaller vertical chimney hole cutting skyward through a boulder

Fat Man's & Lady's Misery - Narrow passageways between mammoth boulders, at 4 separate places

Tangerine Squeeze - a relative of Fat Man's Misery at the other end of the Glen

Balancing Rocks - Two huge boulders perched precariously on the edge of the cliffs overlooking the Niagara River.

Leaning Rock - huge slab of limestone lying in a slanted position

Sentinel Rock - A 50-foot high rectangular boulder perched on a steep bank at the edge of the Glen, overlooking the Niagara River 100 feet below. You can climb to its airy, but flat top for an exhilarating experience.

Indian Shelter - a ledge overhang that forms a grotto that has been used for centuries for campfires

Air Conditioner Grotto - a small rock enclosure with cold air pouring out of it

<u>Devil's Hole Rapids</u>: The churning whitewater portion of the Niagara River that flows past the Glen. Standing waves reach 5 feet high. The trail reaches it at several places.

Remember to take a pair of binoculars and a camera.

Caution: Take extreme care near the edge of the river or cliffs. Rocks near the river are often slippery and the currents are treacherous. Do not swim!

Directions:

The Driving Route: From Buffalo, take Rt. 190 north to Niagara Falls, and then the Robert Moses parkway to downtown Niagara Falls. Cross into Canada by the Rainbow Bridge. From Hamilton and Toronto, take the Queen Elizabeth Way to Rt. 420, following signs to Niagara Falls and the Rainbow Bridge. From points south of Buffalo, take the NY Thruway (Rt. 90) east to Buffalo, then Rt. 190 north to Niagara Falls via the Robert Moses Parkway. From Rochester and points east, take the NY Thruway west to Rt. 290 west which takes you to Rt. 190 north to Niagara Falls.

Once on the Canadian side of the Rainbow Bridge, turn north along the Niagara Parkway, the road that parallels the Niagara River downstream. As you leave the city area, watch for the

Whirlpool Restaurant/Golf Course. About 0.7 mile/1.2 km. further, you will see the sign for "Christmas in the Gardens Shop" on your right, which is where parking for Niagara Glen Park is (why they don't identify the Glen with a sign is beyond me!). It is about 3.5 miles/5.8 km. from the Rainbow Bridge. Pull into the parking lot near the shop and park your car. Read the mounted trail map.

The Hiking Route: Descend into the picnic area and walk by the picnic shelter straight toward the gorge edge. At the edge, turn left and walk until you reach the metal stair entrance that leads down the imposing staircase to the bottom of the cliff. From the bottom of the stair, walk straight ahead, following the cliff face in a downstream direction. The white-blazed trail will descend down rock steps through a jumble of mammoth angular chunks of rock that fell from the top of the cliff centuries or millennia ago.

When you reach the bottom of the steps, you will be at a trail junction with the Red and Blue Trails. Notice the ever-present roar of the Niagara River's rapids. Turn right down the Red Trail about 50 feet and then detour down the Blue Trail to your left to get a look at the Twin Potholes. One hundred feet past the junction with the Red Trail is the first 4-foot step down a ledge. Then the trail curves and loops to the right and the trail drops down a second sudden step (a blue-blazed tree marks this point) as it skirts around a slanted slab of limestone. This is where the **Twin Pot Holes** are. As you step down, look *backward* at the face of the slab and you will see two-foot wide "eyes" staring upward. **Turn around and go back to the Red Trail now.** Otherwise you may miss the choice route for seeing all the curious rock formations. On your way back up, notice a chimney-like rock on your left.

Twenty feet before the junction with the Red Trail, you will notice a path cuts off to the left. A few feet in, you will see the **Indian Shelter** under a massive boulder. Notice its grotto ceiling is blackened from hundreds of campfires over the centuries.

Take the Red Trail to the left. Admire the peacefulness of this mature forest. Angular boulders lie everywhere and in every possible position. Try to imagine what it was like when each one crashed down from the cliff above. Notice the lush growth of ferns, mosses and delicate wildflowers.

The trail will descend a wooden stairs. Halfway down, notice the tall, rounded pothole impression carved vertically into the rock face to your left. A ways further, the trail will lead you through one and then another narrow space between boulders referred to as **Fat Man's Misery**. Under the second, stop under the rock overhang and look for **Fat Man's Pothole**, a hole through which you can see the sky. (Between the two Fat Man Miseries, the Green Trail cuts off to the left -- ignore it.)

Shortly after, you'll come to a broad, flat wall on a boulder. Notice the **cave** in it. Next, you'll see **Leaning Rock**, followed a little later by **Fat Lady's Misery**. Right after that is the "big mama" of pot holes: **Devil's Oven**, located on the underside of a boulder the trail passes. About 5 feet wide and ten feet long, it can be climbed to reach its upper end, which faces skyward.

The trail continues to weave among rock chunks (including one circle path that takes you back to the same trail a little further). Then you will come to the "big mama" of boulders: **Sentinel Rock**. You'll approach it from below and it will tower over you strikingly. It will be hard to believe, but in a few moments, you'll be climbing to the top of it! Follow the trail and it will climb up and around the rock until you reach a flat area just below its pinnacle. The summit will appear like a ten-foot wall but it can be climbed by holding onto hand and foot holds. The effort will be worth it. The top is relatively flat with a commanding bird's eye view over the entire Niagara Gorge. Plan to have lunch there.

When you leave Sentinel Rock, the Red Trail will take you toward the Escarpment cliffs and will finally end at the Green Trail. Turn left on the Green Trail. Along the way, you will pass 1) **Air Conditioner Grotto**, from which cool air flows out (on your right), 2) a small **cave** on your left, 3) the rock cleft **Lemon Squeeze**, and 4) a long wooden staircase. At the bottom of the stairs is a sign "Trail Closed" but if you go past it a short distance, you'll see a large **rock shelter** under a 15-foot overhang. Park authorities appear to be trying to discourage partying youths from camping out here and littering the site with broken bottles. Return to the Green Trail and continue descending all the way to the Niagara River. (Ignore the Yellow Trail you'll pass along the way.)

Finally, you will reach the river at **Cripp's Eddy**, a relatively quiet, protected cove of the river that is popular with anglers. Notice the tide-like waves and surges of water onto the shore that remind one more of an *ocean* shore than a river shore. Remember, the Niagara River is not like other rivers. Just upstream is the treacherous Whirlpool and the violent Whirlpool Rapids. The currents down here are still affected by this incredible churning of water. Note that a trail continues upstream past Cripps Eddy until it reaches the impressive Whirlpool Basin. You may want to plan to take this route at another time. In the meantime, our route will take you through more of the Niagara Glen to see the rest of its delights.

From Cripp's Eddy, follow the trail along the shore in a downstream direction (from looking at the river, you will have no problem deciding what way is downstream!). Soon, you will notice the blue blazes. You will pass several views over the river, as well as a Yellow Trail coming in from the left. A ways further on the Blue Trail, you will come upon two giant boulders called **Balancing Rocks**. One is perched on a narrow base and the other is perched on the cliff edge over the roaring river. (Another section of Yellow Trail intersects here.)

A few feet after Balanced Rocks, go to the cliff edge and look for where a rough path climbs below the ledge over rocks down to the river. While you could continue on the Blue Trail, this is a much more fascinating alternate, though more difficult, route -- which will bring you back up to the Blue Trail anyway. Climb down this route and you will end up among boulders beneath a striking vertical, overhanging ledge. If you wish, you may climb right down to the river over boulders to experience the **Devil's Hole Rapids** at eye level. Notice how they are much more impressive at river level than further up. **Exercise strong caution here since the currents are lethal!** As you continue along the bottom of the ledge, you will see a spring that pours out of a crevice under the ledge. The water is clear and cold, but should not be drunk since chemicals from industry above the gorge are capable of seeping through the limestone through cracks. A little further ahead and you will climb back up to the Blue Trail.

Continue downstream on the Blue Trail, which will be smooth and easy. You'll pass several river views and the Green Trail and a Blue Trail on your left. Continue to stay along the river. When you reach the Red Trail on your left, turn onto it. This end of the Red Trail will take you through a quiet, seldom-travelled stretch of mature, attractive forest called **Foster Flats**. It will parallel a high rocky ridge to your left, which blocks much of the sound of the river. The peaceful setting gives you no clue to the sudden change in landscape you are about to encounter.

Suddenly, you will pass through the **Tangerine Squeeze** (like Fat Man's Misery). Then you skirt by **Giant Window Shelter** to your right. Climb into it to its other opening. The trail takes you next past a rock cul-de-sac on your right. At its end is a step-down **Frigid Crevice** with refrigerated air flowing from it, a great refresher on a hot day. Following that, you

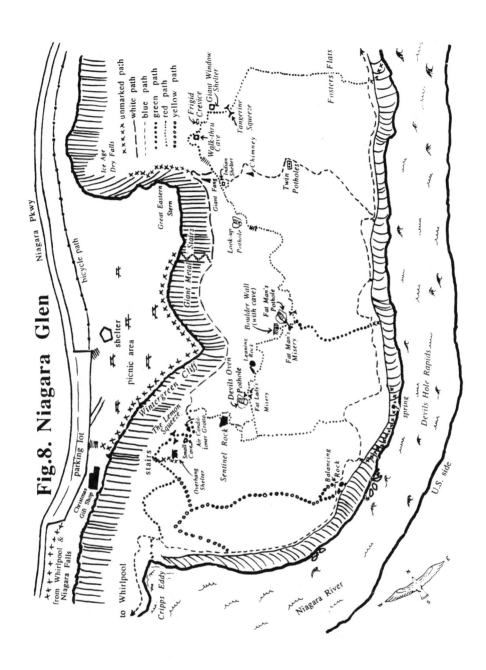

Fig.8. Niagara Glen

unmarked path
white path
blue path
green path
red path
yellow path

Niagara Pkwy

bicycle path

parking lot

Christmas Gift Shop

from Whirlpool & Niagara Falls

to Whirlpool

Cripps Eddy

Niagara River

stairs

Overhang Shelter

Small Cave

Air Conditioner Grotto

The Lemon Squeeze

Wintergreen Cliff

Sentinel Rock

Devils Oven

Pothole

Fat Lady's Misery

Leaning Rock

Balancing Rock

Fat Man's Misery

Fat Man's Pothole

Boulder Wall (with cave)

Look-up Pothole

Giant Metal Stairs

Great Eastern Stern

Ice Age Dry Falls

shelter

picnic area

Giant Fang

Indian Shelter

Chimney

Walk-thru Cave

Frigid Crevice

Tangerine Squeeze

Giant Window Shelter

Fosters Flats

Twin Potholes

spring

Devils Hole Rapids

U.S. side

N
E
S
W

pass through a large **cave-like rock enclosure** and out the other side. A flight of steps takes you up suddenly and shortly after that, you are back to the original Red, White and Blue trail junction that you started from! (The trail colors might remind some of the American flag, but you're in Canada. However, the Glen's sugar maple forest is abundant with "Mapleleafs" -- how fitting, eh?)

Take the White Trail up the stone steps to the cliffs and the metal staircase to the parking lot.

Between giant boulders in Niagara Glen

MERRITT ISLAND, WHERE THE RIVER FLOWS UNDER THE CANAL

A tranquil, weeping willow-lined bicycle or foot trail that traverses a long narrow island surrounded on both sides by blue-green waters, one the Welland River, the other the Welland Canal. At the upper and lower end of the island, the Welland River can be seen where it literally flows *under* the Welland Canal ! In fact, this "Secret Place" gives you the opportunity to travel *between* a canal and a river, *over* a river that goes *under* a canal (twice), and even a way to drive your car *under* the canal. It won't make you famous or get you in the Guinness Book of World Records, but it will provide fun conversation when you're with your friends. To enrich your experience even more, you can do a walking tour of the city of Welland and see two dozen giant murals painted on buildings, each depicting a different scene of history.

Distance: 2.4 to 6 miles/4 to 10 km. of bicycling or walking, depending on choice of route.

Difficulty: Easy

Notable Features:

Merritt Island Park: Three-mile/5 km. long finger of an island bound on either side by the blue-green colored Welland Canal and the Welland River. This well-kept city park has a tranquillity that is hard to match in any other semi-urban park. Bird life is abundant. Picnic, boating, playground and athletic facilities are provided in the park, which is a block from Welland's downtown.

Merritt Trail: The 27 mile/45 kilometer hiking and biking trail that parallels the Welland Canal or its associated waterways from Port Dalhousie on Lake Ontario to Port Colbourne on Lake Erie. A 2.4 mile/4 km. side trail of the Merritt Trail, called the Welland Canal Parkway, follows the length of Merritt Island and is the focus of this "Secret Place." It is paved and lined with willows, maples, apple trees and benches. A parallel, unpaved trail follows the river side of the island to offer an alternate return route.

Welland Canal. The shipping canal built to bypass Niagara Falls. It takes ships up or down 326 feet/99 m. through eight locks

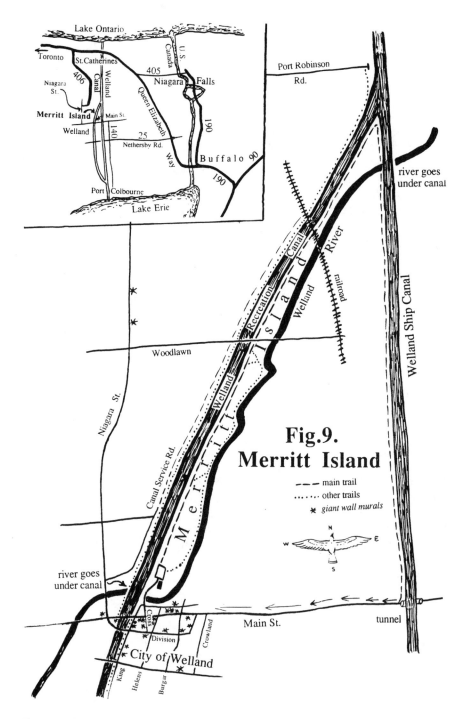

Fig.9.
Merritt Island

- - - main trail
...... other trails
* giant wall murals

Lake Ontario

Toronto

St.Catherines

Niagara St.

Merritt Island

Welland

Welland Canal

406

140

25

Nethersby Rd.

Main St.

Canada

U.S.

405

Niagara Falls

Queen Elizabeth Way

190

190

Buffalo

90

Port Colbourne

Lake Erie

Port Robinson Rd.

river goes under canal

Recreation Canal

Island

Welland River

railroad

Welland Ship Canal

Woodlawn

Niagara St.

Canal Service Rd.

Merritt

river goes under canal

Main St.

tunnel

Cross

Division

Crowland

City of Welland

King

Helens

Burgar

to transport them between Lakes Erie and Ontario. Four canal sections were built, the first in 1829, the last in 1973. The section on the west shore of Merritt Island was built in 1932 and is now a recreational waterway for pleasure craft and water sports only.

Two road tunnels take the city of Welland's Main Street and Town Line Road under the canal. They cost $46 million to construct in 1973.

Welland River. The east-west river that drains much of Ontario's Niagara Peninsula. Since the Welland Canal was cut in a north-south route, a way had to be found to accomplish the implausible: to route the river *under* the canal. Not just once, but twice! As one enters Merritt Island, the road crosses over where the river quietly flows into an aqueduct under the wider canal -- not an exciting event, but very curious! It exits on the other side of the canal. The same crossing is made at the opposite end of the island. Canoeists can often be seen on the river.

The Giant Historical Murals of Welland. In 1988, the city of Welland decided to turn itself into a colorful outdoor art gallery, open 12 months a year -- and free. There are 24 murals along downtown streets, most of them along a five-block stretch. Some are more than 60 feet long, others 3 stories high. Conveniently, they are located right next to Merritt Island and add one more unique and fascinating feature to this "Secret Place."

Some examples of the mural scenes are:
> An 19th century scene of horses on the towpath
> > pulling a ship through the canal
> A winter scene of the Welland area
> A band concert in a park in 1910
> Mid-1900s scenes at the Welland Fair
> Night scene and reflections on the glistening canal
> The world's largest paint-by-number mural (!),
> > painted by 1000 people in 1989 to celebrate
> > the ethnic diversity of Welland

Directions:

From Hamilton, Toronto and other Ontario points to the west, take Queen Elizabeth Way east to St. Catherines and exit onto Rt. 406. Take it to its end at Niagara Street in Welland. From Niagara Falls, New York, take the Peace Bridge into Niagara Falls, Ontario. In Niagara Falls, Ontario, take Rt. 420 to Lundy's Lane which becomes Rt. 20. Take Rt. 20 to Rt. 406 south and take 406 to its end at Niagara Street in Welland. Turn left on Niagara Street and then left on Main Street. Cross the bridge over the canal and take a left onto Cross Street.

From Buffalo and other points east and south in the U.S., cross into Canada and take Queen Elizabeth Way to Exit 12 - Netherby Road. Turn right on Rt. 140 and take it to Main Street. Turn left onto Main Street west into downtown Welland. Once in downtown Welland, turn right at Cross Street. If you reach the bridge over the canal, go back two blocks.

Follow Cross Street across the little bridge over the Welland River-under-the-Welland-Canal crossing, and continue to the end of the last parking lot.

From the parking lot, pass through the gate at the further end and begin your bicycle or walking trip. Note that a detailed map is on a kiosk in front of the recreational center building. The paved trail proceeds 3 km. to a railroad crossing. After checking for trains, cross the tracks and continue ahead on what has turned into a gravel trail. You are now in an open landscape. Follow it to where it turns sharply to the right and you will reach the main Welland Shipping Canal. Follow the trail to where the Welland River makes its other crossing under the canal.

From here, if you are hiking or bicycling, you can return the same way you came (10 km.). On your way back down the island, pass the boat dock on the canal and watch for a paved trail that cuts off on the left and leads to the parallel gravel path along the Welland River. It will give you a change of scenery on your last stretch home. You will know this fork because it points in the direction of where your car is. Any paved fork that points toward the opposite end of the island is a nature trail not suitable for bicycles.

If you are bicycling, you can instead choose an alternate route home. It is 3 km. longer and less scenic, but gives you a "circle" route and an experience of the active shipping canal.This route continues on the gravel road along the main shipping canal until it reaches Main Street. Note the auto tunnel to your left as it crosses under the 27-foot/10 meter-deep canal.Turn right on Main Street and in 3 km., you will be in downtown Welland.

Using your map, you can bike or walk around town to see all the giant murals before returning up Cross Street to your car.

DECEW FALLS, ROCKWAY FALLS
AND THE FALLS THAT TURNS ON AND OFF

Views of two high waterfalls and one strange falls that turns on and off! Connecting these is an enjoyable hike through scenic Ontario woodlands along the Niagara Escarpment. Add to your menu of scenic delights two caves, a historic operating mill and museum, four smaller waterfalls, and a scenic drive past two historic homes and grape vineyards with wine tasting.

Distance: 4.9 miles/8.1 km. hiking one way, if a two-car option is used; an additional 5 miles/8.3 km. of bicycling if the hike-and-bike option is chosen; it is a round trip of 9.8 miles/16.3 km. of hiking if only one car is used.

Difficulty: Easy to moderate. However, if you choose the optional adventurous climb down into Decew Falls' gorge, this portion is short but challenging.

Options: This Secret Place gives you several options: 1) hike along the Bruce Trail from Decew Falls to Rockway Falls and hike back, 2) bicycle both ways, 3) hike to Rockway and bicycle back, 4) hike to Rockway and drive your car back, 5) just use your car to get from one falls to the other. The directions and special arrangements are described further ahead.

Notable Features:

Decew Falls: 60-foot/18 meter high falls with a 20-foot/6 meter overhanging ledge. It plunges into a rather inaccessible gorge. A historic mill (still operating since 1872!) and museum (Mountain Mills Museum) sit just behind its crest. The falls and mill are in a St. Catherines city park.

A view of the upper half of Decew Falls can be seen from a spot behind the old mill, but it is best seen from its bottom, where the entire plunge, fascinating cliff overhang, and impressive rock amphitheatre can be appreciated. However, this requires taking the challenging option of climbing into the gorge. It is also the only way to see Faucet Falls, the Cave/Tunnels and Lower Decew Falls.

Faucet Falls: A bizarre waterfall only 300 feet downstream from Decew Falls. It drops 40 ft./12 m. out of a cave opening in the gorge wall, and flows heavy every half hour or so, then reduces

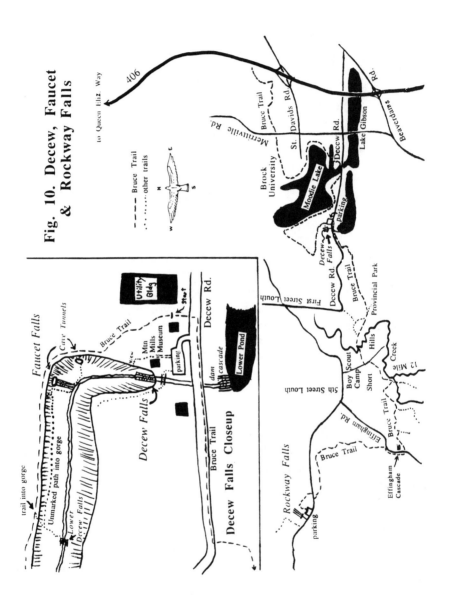

Fig. 10. Decew, Faucet & Rockway Falls

— — — Bruce Trail
· · · · · · other trails

to a trickle, then starts up again! Can you figure out its weird behavior and source?

Cave/Tunnels. Two cave tunnels mid-way up the wall of Decew Falls gorge. Faucet Falls flow out of one cave, whose opening cannot be entered because a metal grate prevents access. The other cave opening can be entered if you bring flashlights and boots to deal with the very shallow pools of water on the floor.

Rockway Falls: Scenic 130-foot falls that drops into a yawning canyon seen from vista overlooks off the Bruce Trail. The city of Toronto 35 miles across Lake Ontario can also be seen on a clear day. The falls is the endpoint for this suggested hike.

Four Other Waterfalls. Three more waterfalls can easily be seen, and one more requires a challenging climb into the gorge:

Lower Decew Falls. This 25-foot falls is impressive in its own right, but is very difficult to get to. It can be reached by the same route that descends into the gorge to get to Faucet Falls, the Cave/Tunnels and the bottom of Decew Falls.

Lower Reservoir Cascade. Easily seen from the parking lot for Decew Falls/Morningstar Mill Park, this graceful 25-foot drapery of water is actually artificial. It is the overflow from the Lower Reservoir that serves as the drinking water source for the City of St. Catherines. Its flow is good year-round.

Effingham Cascade. Just as you exit Short Hills Provincial Park by the Bruce Trail, you can see a 15-foot cascade. It is best seen during spring, since it can totally dry up during the summer months.

Lower Rockway Falls. In addition to the tall Rockway Falls, one can see its smaller 20-foot high sister from one of the clifftop lookouts off the Bruce Trail overlooking Rockway gorge.

The best time to visit all seven falls is March to early July, when the flow is greatest, and then again from late September into winter, when dramatic ice formations form. In the summer, the falls can reduce to a trickle.

Short Hills Provincial Park. Part of the suggested hike between Decew and Rockway Falls traverses the northern part of this new park. Its 1700 acres (700 hectares) encompass young and mature woodlands interspersed with wildlife-filled, secluded meadows, brooks and ravines. Nine waterfalls drop off exposed faces of the Niagara Escarpment. These flow well only during spring and after rainy periods. A complex network of trails traverse the park, including the famous Bruce Trail. The park's many rounded hills form a U-shaped pattern projecting south from the normal east-west orientation of the Niagara Escarpment. They were created when the great Ice Age glaciers overlaid this region. At one point during a melting period, torrential floods of meltwaters flowed off the glacier, forming a floodway which carved this U-shaped valley into the Niagara Escarpment.

Bruce Trail: See description under Tews Falls.

Niagara Escarpment: The 1400-mile long cliff or bluff that runs from Rochester, NY, through the Province of Ontario, along the northern edge of two Great Lakes and then into southeastern Wisconsin. Made of limestone and dolomite, dozens of waterfalls drop off this high ledge, including the most famous -- Niagara Falls.

Directions:

From New York State, the NY Thruway (Rt. 90) will take you to Rt. 190 north to Niagara Falls, which is well-marked on highway signs. Cross the customs station and into Canada and take Queen Elizabeth Way west. From Hamilton and other cities in Ontario, take Queen Elizabeth Way east.

From Queen Elizabeth Way, exit off the Rt. 406 exit in St. Catherines. Take Rt. 406 south to St. Davids Rd exit. Turn west on St. Davids Rd (Rt. 71), toward Brock University. Go to the next 4-way intersection and turn left onto Merrittville Highway (Rt. 50). (If you enter Brock University, you've gone too far.) Take the next right turn (Decew Rd.). Pass along the shore of Moody Reservoir. Watch on the right for the sign for Mountain Mills Museum. Park in the lot. (If you descend a very steep, winding road, you've gone too far.)

Decew Falls can be seen by walking behind the old mill via the driveway that leads from the parking lot. The view through the fence, unfortunately, is not an ideal full view. Another option is to cross the creek 30 feet *upstream* from the falls by walking the concrete wall that crosses the creek and then walking through the woods toward a full view of the falls. **Remember, safety should be followed when crossing the stream or when near cliffs.**

Faucet Falls can be partially seen from the viewpoint into the gorge that is across the stream from the mill. Look downstream from Decew Falls along the cliff face on the right (east) side of the river. The falls drops out of a cave midway up the cliff. If you see and hear nothing, you are between flow cycles (which average every half hour). Otherwise, it will be very obvious. However, the only way to get a *closeup* view of this odd falls, as well as the cave/tunnels and Lower Decew Falls, is by descending into the bottom of the gorge. This is also the ideal way to see the larger Decew Falls and its rock overhang.

Descending into the gorge is a challenging adventure, and not for the faint of heart or small children. It involves hand-over-hand climbing down one 7-foot rock face, walking along narrow ledges, and scrambling up and down steep, loose-rock slopes. But it is very rewarding! To do it, start from the parking lot and walk 150 feet up the road away from the stream until you see a white blaze on a tree to your left, next to a gate. (A long, low utility building lies on the other side of the gate.) A wooden ladder (a style) enables you to climb over the fence. The white blazes mark the Bruce Trail. The trail will take you past a couple of partial views of Decew Falls, then it will turn to the left, following the edge of the gorge. After it enters the woods, watch carefully for a red trail blaze on a tree on the *right* side of the trail, which marks the descent route on your *left*. The route appears as a bare soil, well-trodden break in the otherwise dense vegetation that lines the cliff edge. **Remember, you must see the red paint blaze to be certain of the correct descent route.** (Also, shortly after this point, the main trail leaves the woods and enters open field.)

Follow the route down over the rock steps for 20 feet and you will then be standing atop a 7-foot ledge. While it may look difficult to descend, it has good hand- and footholds in a crevice. At the bottom of this ledge, follow the narrow, rough path upstream. (Do not descend to the bottom of the gorge.) Soon, you will reach **Faucet Falls**. To get a look into its **cave**, walk very carefully along the very narrow ledge that leads to it, which is wet and can be slippery (**Caution!**) When you look inside between the bars of the gate, notice there is another waterfall visible in the light at the end of the tunnel. (Did you ever wonder what was really in "the light at the end of the tunnel"? Well, here's the answer!)

To get to the bottom of Decew Falls, descend the steep "path" to the side of Faucet Falls. Take caution since the gravel slides easily. Once at the bottom, walk to the falls. Notice the overhang, the vines hanging down, the mist, the historic stone mill next to it. If it's summertime, take a dip in the plunge pool. You'll appreciate it because the climb back up will start you sweating again.

The second **cave/tunnel** is located between Faucet and Decew Falls, half way up the cliff. There is an obvious path leading up to it. You can enter the cave tunnel, which is fortified with cinder blocks just inside. The pools of water are shallow and will not stop you from exploring it with flashlights.

The spot in front of the cave provides a good and different view of both falls. It is a good spot to eat lunch, which will also give you time to observe the changes in Faucet Falls. If you're lucky, you may see it reduce to a trickle or a light flow, or suddenly change to heavy flow. Do we have your curiosity up?

Before you leave, please pick up any cans and trash so as to keep the site scenic.

To see **Lower Decew Falls**, you can bushwhack 1000 feet down the stream until you reach it, or you can return exactly the same way you came. This second option is more climbing but less pushing your way through dense vegetation. For the second option, climb back up to Faucet Falls and follow the bottom of the ledge till you reach the cliff route up to the top. When you reach this point, however, head *down* the rough path below. It will quickly take you to the crest of Lower Decew Falls. This is a beautiful and seldom-visited spot. If you want to see the falls from its bottom, you'll have to find your own way -- there's not even a hint of a route. But at least you've come this far!

To return to the top of the gorge, climb back up the rolly-polly gravel path to the cliff face and back to the marked Bruce Trail. Take the trail back to the parking lot.

Now that you have seen Decew and Faucet Falls, you can complete this adventure by visiting Rockway Falls. If you have chosen Option 1,2 or 3 on page 39, you can start right from the parking lot. If you choose Option 3, to hike to Rockway and bike back, you need to get your bicycle(s) dropped off at Rockway Falls and then drive back to Decew. At Rockway Falls' parking lot, there is a perfect place to chain your bikes up. Large cement blocks line the back of the parking lot; each one has a cable loop perfect for securing your bicycle. If you choose Option 4, to hike to Rockway and drive back, you will need to bring two cars so that you can first drop one off at Rockway's parking lot and then shuttle back to Decew with the other car.

Trail Sense: There are many places on the route between Decew and Rockway (and elsewhere along the Bruce Trail) where the trail cuts off suddenly into the woods or up a hill. If one is not paying attention, it is easy to pass these turnoffs and get off-track.

The **Bruce Trail** is marked along its entire length by white squares or spots painted on trees, posts or boulders. However, you can accidently walk off the Bruce Trail onto a side trail if you fail to notice the white blazes at these critical intersections. This mistake can, at the least, cause you to have to walk longer and be delayed, and at the worst, cause you to get disoriented.

To avoid this, always follow this rule: *the person in the lead always looks for every trail blaze along the route and notes when a blaze has not been noticed for several hundred feet.* Trail blazes occur on the average of every 50 to 150 feet (and often closer over complicated terrain). If you don't notice a blaze after a while, you may have passed a turnoff. In that case, backtrack along the trail to find the last trail blaze. From that point, walk forward on the trail again, carefully looking for blazes. Sometimes, a tree that has a blaze on it has fallen, or leaves have obscured the blaze. In other cases, the trail has turned off or forked at a not-so-easily-noticed spot. Trail intersections or sudden turns are always marked with two blazes, one diagonally over the other. The direction that the blazes are leaning tells you the direction that the trail is turning. This is vital to remember!

Directions for Hiking to Rockway Falls: From the Decew Falls parking lot, walk onto Decew Road, turn right and walk along the road for 0.25 mile. A little way past the creek, you will notice a yard with a long wooden rail fence on your left. At the far end of that fence, the Bruce Trail turns off along the edge of a field. Take care to watch for this point, which is marked on your left by two white blazes. If the road suddenly starts to descend down a hill, you have passed the trail turnoff.

Note: bring insect repellant during the summer and proper footware for possibly muddy conditions at the bottom of the valley during spring.

The trail will pass through beautiful woods and meadows filled with songbirds and wildflowers. You will quickly forget about civilization as you traverse the northern part of **Short Hills Provincial Park**. The trail will interweave with a blue-blazed trail and other paths (at least five intersections), but you stay on the white trail. You will then cross a footbridge across Twelve Mile Creek. About 800 feet after the creek crossing, you will come upon a gravel road (which leads to Witaskiwin Boy Scout Camp). The trail will follow the road to the left for only 100 feet before cutting back into the woods on your right (look for this point!). Soon the white-blazed Bruce Trail will join with a yellow trail and the blue trail will continue off to your left. Stay on the white trail and you will soon follow along the creek, enter another large scrubby meadow, then travel within sight of the creek again.

Shortly after leaving the creek area, the Bruce Trail will suddenly cut off to the right, with the yellow trail (the wider one) continuing ahead. (Don't miss this point!) The Bruce Trail will gradually climb uphill out of the broad valley carved by the Ice Age glacier's floodwaters. You will pass two more path intersections before finally reaching Effingham Road. Fifty feet before the road, check out the brook and its waterfall (**Effingham Cascade**) to your right (it may be dried up in summer).

Once you reach Effingham Road, the trail follows it to the right for a couple hundred meters. Watch for double trail blaze on the opposite side of the road just past a house. It enters a grassy corridor through woods and shortly after reaches a large field. At the entrance to the field, *turn right* and skirt the field to the other side to locate the white blaze in a narrow break in the woods. This trail can be hard to see in midsummer when weeds have grown high. It crosses several styles over fences, passes a few horse farms and then follows an old woods road for a short distance. Watch carefully on your left where the double blaze indicates where the trail suddenly turns sharp left up the steep wooded slope to the top of the escarpment. Note the exposed limestone blocks and crevices along the top of the hill.

When you reach Pelham Road, walk across it and turn right. Pass through a small field, more woods, a small creek and a side trail before reaching the edge of Rockway Falls Gorge. Here, several lookout points will reward you with a dramatic vista of the gorge, **Rockway Falls**, the smaller **Lower Rockway Falls**, and a panorama of Lake Ontario. On a clear day, Toronto can be seen 41 miles/63 km. away!

After enjoying the vista, you will reach the parking lot behind the Rockway Community Center. Here, you can hike, bike or drive back, according to which option you chose. If you bike or drive back, take Pelham Road past Effingham Road and the Boy

Scout Camp entrance, then make the next right to Decew Road down the steep hill to Decew Falls. Note the historic homes and wineries along the way.

Decew Falls

DEVIL'S PUNCHBOWL AND ALBION FALLS

Visit two very contrasting waterfalls: one with a high vertical drop into a rugged canyon amphitheatre, the other one gentle and nestled in a quiet vale with a lazy, leisurely ambience in summer and fall. Perfect for dipping your feet -- or your entire body. Dramatic panoramas and other waterfalls complete the delightful effect.

Distance: 1.2 miles/2 km. of walking for the easy option; 6 miles/10 km of hiking for the longer option.

Difficulty: Easy or moderately difficult, depending on the choice.

Options: The easy option is to take separate short walks into three parks with waterfalls. Each park is connected by a short car drive. The longer option is to hike the Bruce Trail from one park to the other. To avoid making the longer option *even* longer, the two-car shuttle method is recommended to avoid having to walk back the same 6 mile/10 km. route you came.

Notable Features:

Devil's Punch Bowl and Falls: This impressive waterfall makes an airy plunge of 111 feet/34 meters off an overhanging ledge into the Devil's Punchbowl, a vertical-walled semicircular rock amphitheatre. It is located in a park with a sweeping panorama over Hamilton and Lake Ontario. Toronto can be seen 38 miles/53 km. away on a clear day. Best time to see the falls is May and June; it sometimes dries up in the heat of mid-summer.
One can stay at the top for the vistas, or add the challenging option of climbing down into the canyon to view Devils Punchbowl Falls from the bottom.
Albion Falls: A 69-foot/21 meter high cascade that drops down dozens of steps to an area with delightful sunning and wading spots in a gentle, serene setting. A narrow gorge is downstream. Another waterfall, Buttermilk Falls, also drops 69 feet/21 meters into a side ravine, about 0.7 mile/1.2 km. downstream from Albion Falls.
Felker's Falls. An easily accessible 70 foot/22 meter high falls that drops vertically into an isolated rock amphitheatre. Like

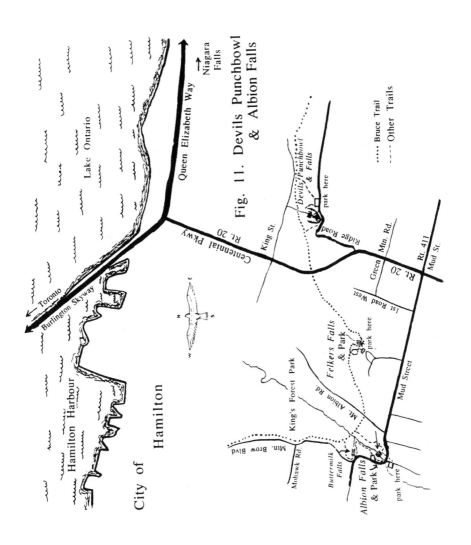

Fig. 11. Devils Punchbowl & Albion Falls

····· Bruce Trail
----- Other Trails

Devils Punchbowl Falls, this falls turns to a trickle in the summer heat. Although the park it lies in is bounded above and below by suburban development, one cannot tell this once on the secluded wooded trail. A beautiful trail loops through mature forest to the falls vista. A plaque on a rock explains why the path is named the "Peter Street Trail" after a local man who inspired those who knew him.

Niagara Escarpment. See Tews Falls description
Bruce Trail. See Tews Falls description

Directions:

From Buffalo and other points in the U.S., cross into Canada and take Queen Elizabeth Way to Hamilton, Ontario. From Toronto and other Ontario cities to the west and north, hook up with Queen Elizabeth Way and take it east.

From Queen Elizabeth Way, exit at Rt. 20 (which is east of the Burlington Skyway Bridge). Take Rt. 20 (Centennial Pkwy.) south through the outskirts of Hamilton and then up the Niagara Escarpment bluff. Upon reaching the top of the bluff, turn left on Ridge Rd. and follow it to the entrance of Devil's Punchbowl Conservation Area.

From the parking lot, walk across the field parallel to the road to see the vista over **Devils Punch Bowl**. The rounded shape of the canyon will explain how it got its name. Then walk along the edge of the canyon away from the road to the vista over Hamilton and Lake Ontario. A large cross is mounted at the vista. See if you can find the Toronto skyline.

If you want to take the vigorous climb to the bottom of the falls, take the path that starts from this vista point. It climbs steeply down. Instead of descending all the way into the bottom of the gorge, descend only 25 feet down and then follow along the base of the uppermost ledge in an upstream direction. You will need to carefully pick your way over the rocks until you come to the falls. If you come in April or May, you may be lucky enough to find a large hill of ice at the base of the falls, the remains of the "ice volcano" or cone that forms every winter from freezing of waterfall mist.

Auto Route to the Other Falls: After seeing Devil's Punchbowl, drive back to Rt. 20 and turn left (south). Take it to Mud Street, where you will turn right (west). Drive 0.9 miles/1.5 km. along Mud Street and you will see a sign "Felker's Falls Conservation Area" directing you to turn right onto Paramount Drive. More signs will direct you to a parking lot.

A 0.5 mile/0.8 km.-long bike/foot trail leads into the woods past the plaque memorial for Peter Street. As you enter the woods, take the left fork in the trail. It will reach the edge of the escarpment and loop you to the right until you reach the vista over **Felkers Falls**. Shortly after that, you will reach the trail that exits you back to your car.

From Felker's Falls, drive back to Mud Street and turn right on it. Drive until Mud Street turns sharply to your left and around a ravine on your right. That is where Albion Falls is. Around the bend, park on your left at the parking lot for Mount Albion Conservation Area and walk across Mud Street to the trail that takes you to the base of **Albion Falls**. Enjoy yourself in this beautiful place!

After enjoying Albion Falls, you can choose to see **Buttermilk Falls**. To do this, walk back up to the road. Follow it across the creek and around the bend to the right until you reach the second parking lot for Mount Albion Conservation Area. From the far end of the parking lot, take the trail. A wider trail leads across fields; a narrower path follows along the edge of the gorge in a downstream direction. Take this path for the more scenic route. Both trails will end up at the same place: a view over a side canyon where Buttermilk Falls drops. This point is only 100 feet from the road. Return by walking along the road to where your car is parked.

Hiking Route to the Other Falls: For the more ambitious, you can hike the Bruce Trail from Devils Punchbowl to Felkers, Albion and Buttermilk Falls. To avoid having to walk back the entire route again, you will need a second car. Drive the second car to Albion Falls and leave it there, then drive the first car back to the Devil's Punchbowl.

From Devil's Punchbowl parking lot, walk along Ridge Road over the creek that drops into the Punchbowl. Then watch for trail markers on your right that indicate where the trail cuts off from the road. The trail will steeply descend the escarpment and join up with the white-blazed Bruce Trail. Turn left (west) on this trail. Soon it will follow a railroad line, which will take you under Rt.20. After this bridge, it will leave the railway, cross a field and enter woods along an abandoned roadway. It will skirt a playing field and waterworks, and enter woods again before skirting the east end of Greenhill Avenue. The trail then gradually climbs to the top of the escarpment where it enters mature woods and the Felker's Falls Conservation Area. It circles an old quarry before reaching Felker's gorge. Finally, it crosses the creek above where it drops over

Felker's Falls and joins with the Peter Street Trail described under the "Auto Route" directions above. Enjoy the vista over the falls.

From here, stay on the white-blazed Bruce Trail. The trail leaves the woods and passes a Town Park's parking lot off Paramount Drive. You will pass a subdivision and then reach Mount Albion Road. After crossing the road, the trail traverses a field and then descends a wooded slope into the City of Hamilton's King Forest Park. Watch for a marked side trail to your left (the Mt. Albion Side Trail). If you come to a sizable creek (Redhill Creek, the one that drops over Albion Falls upstream), you have passed the side trail. Take the side trail up to Albion Falls and to your second car. If the weather is warm, be sure to enjoy cooling yourself at the falls!

Graceful Albion Falls

TEWS FALLS, WEBSTERS FALLS AND SPENCER GORGE WILDERNESS

Visit a hidden, wilderness canyon at the doorstep of the City of Hamilton, Ontario, with some of the most dramatic waterfalls in the Niagara region. You can also see the Ice Volcano in late winter.

Distance: 1.5 miles/2.5 km., if two cars are used; 3 miles/5 km. if one car is used. Two optional side trips are each 1.5 mi./2.5 km.

Difficulty: Easy to moderate. The optional bushwhack sidetrip is strenuous.

Notable Features:

Spencer Gorge Wilderness Park: A wild, seemingly inaccessible canyon wilderness just outside the edge of Hamilton, Ontario. It is 240 feet/73 meters deep. Tews and Webster's Falls are part of this park.

Tews Falls: **One of the highest unbroken vertical drops (134 feet/41 meters) of any of the 400 waterfalls in the Niagara Region.** The view of this breathtaking plunge is awesome from the overlook platform or from below.

Webster's Falls: **The Niagara Peninsula's largest waterfall** (greatest flow) other than Niagara Falls. The 63-foot/19 meter plunge fills its canyon amphitheatre with clouds of mist in spring and early summer. Can be viewed from above and also from its bottom by climbing down an exciting 123-step flight of rock and metal steps. An unforgettable experience can be had in midsummer and early fall when the flow of water is at its lowest. **You can literally walk behind the falls' veil of water, under the overhanging ledge! If done at night, especially with a full moon, the experience is inspiring.** Curtains of water glisten in the moonlight and the whooshing sound of water fills the air, while *you* remain dry.

Bring boots if you plan to walk behind Webster's Falls during low flow season, and a flashlight if you plan to see it at night. Take a raincoat if you plan to walk to the bottom of Webster's Falls during the heavy flow season or to the bottom of Tews Falls.

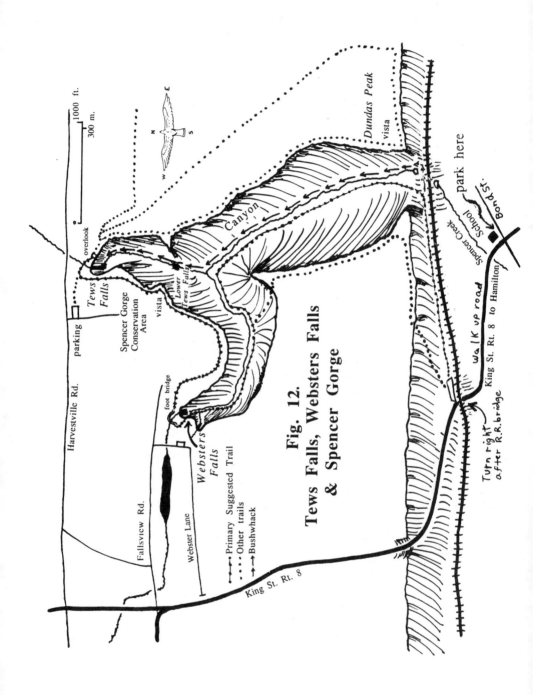

Fig. 12.
Tews Falls, Websters Falls
& Spencer Gorge

1000 ft.
300 m.

N E S W

Dundas Peak
vista

park here

Bond St.

School

Spencer Creek

King St. Rt. 8 to Hamilton

walk up road

Turn right
after R.R. bridge

overlook

Tews Falls

Spencer Gorge
Conservation
Area

parking

Harvestville Rd.

Canyon

vista

Lower
Tews Falls

foot bridge

Websters Falls

Fallsview Rd.

Webster Lane

→ Primary Suggested Trail
···· Other trails
→ Bushwhack

King St. Rt. 8

The Ice Volcano: By late winter, a conical mountain of ice 40 to 100-feet high often forms beneath Tews Falls. It lasts into spring. The waterfall creates the bizarre formation when its spray freezes upon landing as it hits the bottom. The frozen spray builds up higher and higher as it collects more freezing spray. The waterfall continues to carve a cylindrical shaft through it from the top of the cone down to the plunge pool. The stream emerges through an ice cave at its bottom.

Bruce Trail. The world-class hiking trail (*not* named for this author) that follows the Niagara Escarpment (a long limestone ledge or bluff) through southern Ontario from Queenston on the Niagara River to the tip of the Bruce Peninsula that projects into Lake Huron. Of its 464 miles/774 km., 87 miles/146 km. traverse the Niagara Peninsula from Queenston to Hamilton. Along its route are dozens of magnificent vistas and waterfalls, impressive cliffs, parks, caves, streams, beautiful forests and meadows.

Directions:

From the Buffalo area and western New York, cross into Canada via the Peace Bridge from downtown Buffalo or the Lewiston Bridge north of Niagara Falls. Take the Queen Elizabeth Way to the City of Hamilton. Cross over the Burlington Skyway Bridge. After crossing it, get in the *left* lane and watch for Rte. 403 west exit (on the left). From Toronto, take Queen Elizabeth Way to Hamilton and exit onto Rte. 403 west.

Leave Rte. 403 at the Rte. 8 exit. Follow Rte. 8 westward, that is, away from the city. When Rte. 8 (now called King St.) enters Dundas, look for the last street on your right, Bond St. next to a school. <u>If you start driving up a steep stretch and reach a railroad trestle, you've gone too far!</u> After you park, walk up King St. till you reach the railroad trestle. **Walk as far off the road as possible because of dangerous traffic!** After passing under the railroad bridge, turn immediately to the right and onto the right-of-way parallel to the tracks.

From the parking lot, the white-blazed Bruce Trail climbs up the hill slope and passes a viewpoint over the city of Dundas. It follows along the higher part of the slope of **Spencer Gorge Wilderness**. 1.1 mi./1.8 km. from when you started, you will come upon impressive **Webster's Falls**. Just before you see the stone steps, look to your left up a side ravine. If you have gone during the heavy flow period, you will see **Baby Webster Falls** (30 feet high).

Carefully climb among the boulders as close to Webster's Falls as you can. If you have gone during a low flow period, you can probably climb behind the wide curtain of water for an unforgettable experience.

After seeing Webster's Falls from below, ascend the stone and metal steps. Admire the falls from above. The viewing area above is a perfect picnic spot. The park around you is pretty and classically landscaped, including stone arch footbridges. Take the stone footbridge next to you and bear to your right up the trail and around the rim of Webster's gorge. In front of you is a field. Follow its right hand margin until you reach a trail into the woods. This is the same Bruce Trail that you started on. You will pass the gravestones of the Webster family, the original 19th century landowners. The trail takes you through attractive forest, paralleling the edge of Spencer Gorge, with several sweeping vistas.

The trail finally enters a long meadow. Stay on its right margin. At the end of the field, you will see a parking lot near Harvest Road. From the parking lot begins the rest of the trail. Take it to the right and you will reach the overlook platform for **Tews Falls**.

After standing in awe at Tews Falls, you have two opions. You may return back to the car the same way you came, or you may take a 3/4-mile long side trip to a magnificent vista over the City of Hamilton from the edge of the Niagara Escarpment. If you want this option, continue from Tews Falls overlook on the Bruce Trail a

Awe inspiring Tews Falls

short ways along the rim of the gorge and you will reach the junction with the Dundas Peak Side Trail. It will follow along the east edge of Spencer Gorge until it reaches the vista. To return to your car, go back to Tews Falls the same way you came and then follow the entire route you came on.

There are two other variations for visiting Spencer Gorge. If you just want a short, easy walk, you can visit the two waterfalls by parking in the Spencer Gorge Parking Lot. To get there, take King Street (Rt. 8) all the way up the bluff. When Rt. 8 turns sharp left a half-mile later, stay on King Street, straight ahead. At the junction with Harvest Road, turn right. 3/4 mile later, turn right into Spencer Gorge lot, marked with a sign. Here you can get out and walk to both falls. Tews Falls' trail is to your left (when you're facing away from the road) and Webster's Falls' trail is reached by the dirt driveway that heads away from the main road. Hook up with the Bruce Trail from here.

For seasoned bushwhackers, you can go on a wilderness trek to the bottom of Tews Falls, where you can also visit its **Ice Volcano** from February to early April. Follow the directions for the first Spencer Gorge hike by parking your car at the lot next to the railroad tracks. Follow the railroad tracks away from the parking lot until you reach a view of Spencer Gorge from the high railroad embankment. Continue along the tracks until you have crossed to the other side of the stream which lies below. Now, you are on the correct side of Spencer Creek to bushwhack to Tews Falls. Scurry down the steep embankment (no trail) and simply bushwhack your way up the gorge with Spencer Creek to your left. Tews Falls is 0.75 mile/1.25 km. away.

As you get closer to Tews Falls, look for 13-foot/4 m. high **Lower Tews Falls** in the stream to your left. Once you reach Tews Falls, enjoy this rarely seen view from its base. If you are lucky enough to see the Ice Volcano, remember that **it is dangerous to enter or climb it! It can collapse.** With the thundering column of water, the spray and the ice, the scene will look distinctly like you are in Greenland! Bushwhack home the same way you came.

ROYALTON RAVINE RAMBLE

Very pleasant short hike through a scenic wooded valley, across a unique, swinging wooden foot bridge to a waterfall and beautiful picnic spot.

Distance: 2.5 mile round trip

Difficulty: Easy

Notable Features:

Royalton Ravine: Scenic wooded ravine on the edge of the Niagara Escarpment, the same long cliff from which Niagara Falls plunges (see description of the Escarpment under Tews Falls entry).

Swinging Foot Bridge: 80-foot wooden footbridge over a stream. **It may be the longest suspension wooden footbridge in Western New York.** As you cross the bridge, it swings. Kids and kids-at-heart love it because it can be bounced on so that it undulates rhythmically back and forth. Have one person lie in the center of the bridge on his/her back, and have the other person bounce the bridge at one end. The wave motion creates a hilarious sensation! The bridge is only three to six feet above the stream, which is very shallow. Hence, there is little hazard.

Royalton Falls: A 25-foot cascade over the Niagara Escarpment that is a delight to behold. See it in spring, late fall or winter. In mid-summer, it dries to a trickle. Next to it are the remains of an old homestead. The meadow is a perfect place to picnic.

Directions:

From Buffalo, Ontario and points south of Buffalo, take the NY Thruway East to exit 49 (Depew - Rte.78). From Rochester and points east, take the Thruway West to Exit 49. At the end of the exit ramp is Transit Road. Take Transit Road (Rte. 78) north all the way into Niagara County and into Lockport. From Niagara Falls and Ontario, take Rte. 31 from Niagara Falls, NY and drive east into Lockport. From the intersection of Rte. 31 and Rte. 78 in Lockport, travel east on Rte. 31 for 6.5 miles. When it reaches Gasport Road, turn right. Look for Royalton Ravine Park on your right, marked by the sign "Victor Fitchlee Park - Royalton Ravine." Leave your car in the park entrance lot.

the park entrance lot. Walk to the end of the short dirt road past picnic shelters and continue straight across the field ahead of you to the pond. Continue walking with the pond to your left until you reach the edge of the woods. The orange-blazed trail enters attractive, mature forest, then turns left, passing a trail on your right and on the left (this leads you back to the field you just left). It sharply descends a ravine to a brook. **Note:** the color of the trail blazes is changed periodically. If these colors aren't correct, just follow the main trail that <u>bears left and down into the ravine.</u>

The **Swinging Foot Bridge*** is at the bottom of the ravine. After playing on the bridge, continue on and the trail bears left through the valley. <u>It is often muddy along this stretch.</u> Avoid mud by jumping from log to log or skirting the muddy areas. Wildflowers are abundant if you go in May.

The trail bears right and climbs out of the ravine. Soon, it comes to a clearing with the ruins of an old homestead. To the left, a stream flows in a steep ravine below. Just after the house ruins is a trail on the left that takes you to Royalton Falls, only 25 feet from the main trail. It is a great place to picnic. Be sure to visit the ruins, which go back to the 1900s. Return the same route you took.

NOTE: Sometimes, the footbridge is vandalized. If so, call Niagara Co. Parks at 716-439-6040. If you can't cross the stream, you can get to Royalton Falls by driving down Gasport Rd. to Mill St., turn right, drive 1.0 miles to a dirt road (Kayner Rd.) on your right. Drive down it 1/4 mile, park at the gate, and walk on the trail to the falls (see p.60)

The Swinging Foot Bridge in Royalton Ravine

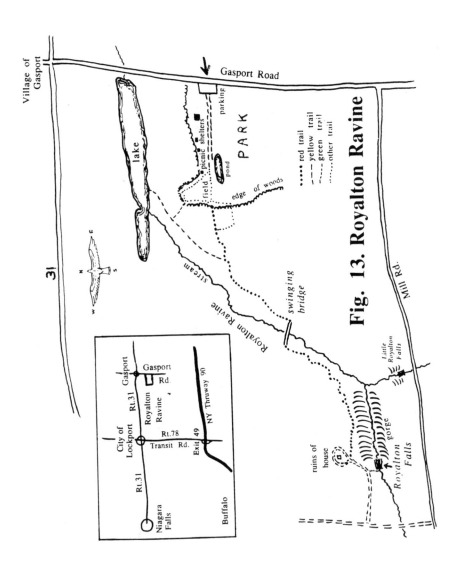

Fig. 13. Royalton Ravine

red trail
yellow trail
green trail
other trail

PARK

Gasport Road

Village of Gasport

31

lake

parking

picnic shelters

field

pond

edge of woods

Royalton Ravine

stream

swinging bridge

Mill Rd.

Little Royalton Falls

gorge

Royalton Falls

ruins of house

City of Lockport

Gasport

Rt.31

Gasport Rd.

Royalton Ravine

Rt.78

Transit Rd.

Exit 49

NY Thruway 90

Rt.31

Niagara Falls

Buffalo

SWALLOW HOLLOW
AND THE FROG ORGY EXPERIENCE

A secluded walk across long boardwalks through a wild wetland, abundant with waterfowl, turtles and frogs. Also, a haunting, night-time walk in spring through amphibious orgies and cacophonous choruses of spring peepers, tree frogs, owls and geese.

Distance: 1 mile loop, with an additional, optional mile on the other side of the road.

Level of Difficulty: Easy

Notable Features:

Iroquois National Wildlife Refuge: At 20,000 acres, the largest wetland and waterfowl habitat in western New York (part of this acreage is in adjoining State Wildlife Areas). It is the remnant of an ancient lake created when the Ice Age glaciers stalled over this area, backing water up.
Swallow Hollow: A public use area and loop trail around and through a wetland and pond in Iroquois National Wildlife Refuge.
The Boardwalk: A 0.6 mile long boardwalk that makes it possible to traverse the wetland in a dry fashion. It is one of the longest boardwalks in Western New York.
The night hike is highly recommended. Most people who experience it never forget it. **The bizarre sounds of singing, peeping and chattering frogs (in a state of orgiastic fervor-- this is their sexual version of "Spring Break") combined with honking geese and hooting owls create a surreal and unique experience.** The night hike is best in late April to early May. Bring flash lights, but use them as little as possible, letting your eyes get used to the sense of night. The best way is to tape a piece of white paper over the flashlight beam to reduce the intensity of the light, but allow you to see the darker parts of the trail. Go only when the temperature is 48 degrees or higher; otherwise the frogs will be relatively quiet.
Of course, a day walk is very worthwhile also. Whether day or night, just **avoid going any time in the summer** unless you enjoy donating your blood to the resident mosquito population!

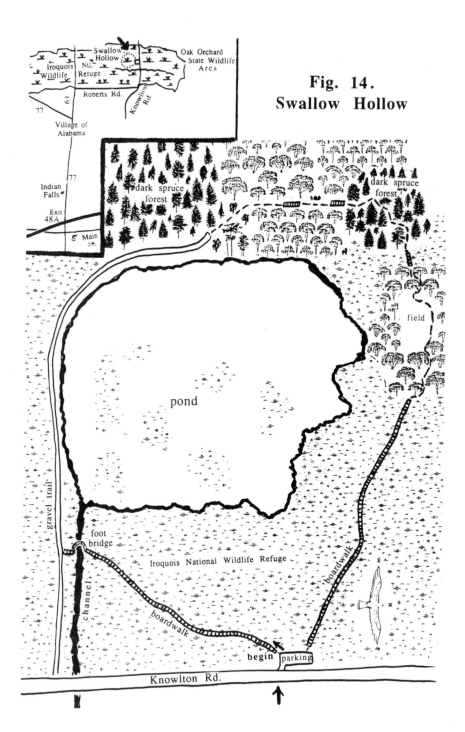

Fig. 14.
Swallow Hollow

Swallow Hollow Ntl. Refuge

Oak Orchard State Wildlife Area

Iroquois Wildlife

Roberts Rd.

Knowlton Rd.

Village of Alabama

77

Indian Falls

77

Exit 48A

5 Main St.

dark spruce forest

dark spruce forest

field

pond

gravel trail

foot bridge

channel

boardwalk

Iroquois National Wildlife Refuge

boardwalk

begin

parking

Knowlton Rd.

Directions:

From the Buffalo area, Ontario, and points south and west, take the NY Thruway (Rt. 90) east to Pembroke Exit 48. From Rochester and points east, take the Thruway west to the same exit.

Take Rt. 77 north. At the village of Alabama, continue straight on 63 N. Look for Roberts Road and turn right (east) on it, skirting the southern edge of the Refuge. (You will know if you passed Roberts Road if Rt.63 takes you into a lonely stretch surrounded on both sides by wetland.) At the end of Roberts Road is Knowlton Road. Turn left (north) and drive 1.8 miles (it is especially important to clock it on your odometer to avoid missing it if you go at night). After you cross a small bridge and river (at the 1.65 mile mark), look for a parking lot entrance road on your left.

Park in the far left corner of the lot. The boardwalk trail begins at that corner. It starts as a long boardwalk over water and wetland. Stop periodically to appreciate the sounds and sense of the place. If you are there at night, turn off flashlights when you pause to allow your eyes to get used to the darkness. The boardwalk will go over a foot bridge to a gravel trail. Turn right and follow it all the way around the pond. Two short sections enter a dark spruce plantation where the trail can be obscure, especially at night. Head straight forward through these trail sections. The trail will soon rejoin a long boardwalk and return to the car.

If you wish, you can take a longer walk. Once back at the parking lot, walk onto the road. Head south to where the creek crosses under the road. Take the trail that heads in on the opposite (left) side of the road. That trail enters the state-owned portion of the wildlife refuge, called Oak Orchard State Wildlife Area. The one-mile trail system winds along board walks, wetlands and across fields and young woods for a very pleasant additional walk. For more trail information for the state wildlife area, call (716)926-2466.

THE ONONDAGA NECKLACE OF WATERFALLS

A waterfall-hopping auto tour of a series of waterfalls -- each with its own personality -- that drop off the Onondaga Escarpment which forms a "necklace" that runs between Buffalo and Rochester. The Devil's Pulpit, a strange mushroom-shaped rock formation, adds diversity to the otherwise splash-filled agenda.

Distance: Four very short walks totalling 0.75 mile

Level of Difficulty: Easy, except the short but steep trail to Morganville Falls.

Notable Features:

Onondaga Escarpment. The 67-mile long dolomite (similar to limestone) rock layer that runs from Buffalo to south of Rochester, paralleling and often underlying the New York State Thruway and Rt. 5. For much of this stretch, it appears as a long, north-facing bluff, ledge or slope. It is the little-known "sister" of the Niagara Escarpment (see description under Decew Falls), which is famous because it forms the precipice that Niagara Falls plunges over. Like the Niagara Escarpment which it parallels 20 miles to the south, the Onondaga Escarpment also has waterfalls that drop off it -- eight of them.

The Escarpment was created more than 400 million years ago at the bottom of an inland sea where lime-secreting organisms grew. The limy layer got compressed into rock and, millions of years later, powerful earth movements gradually lifted the layer toward the surface, while erosion by water stripped off the rock layers above it. The exposed edge of this erosion-resistant layer is what we see today as the escarpment.

Glen Falls.   Nestled into the village center of Williamsville, this picturesque 27-foot high cascade forms a romantic setting in Glen Park. An old red mill, the oldest continuously operating mill (since 1811) in New York State, sits next to the falls, further enhancing its classical appearance. The beautifully landscaped park is popular with families and children and is frequently used for weddings. The falls flows well even in summer.

It is surprising, then, that it took a vigorous citizens' campaign to overcome the opposition of the town board to create the park in the late1970s. Now, this jewel of a park is looked upon

Fig 15. Onondaga Necklace of Waterfalls

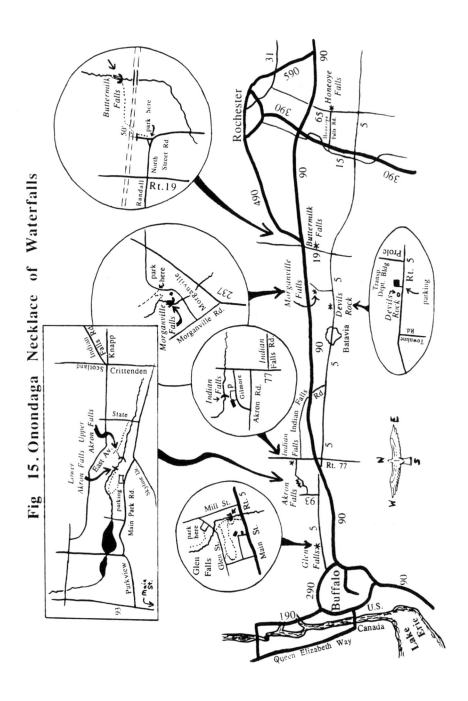

proudly as a special quality of this affluent suburb. It is an example of how the people can be wiser than public officials.

The Willamsville Mill is pleasant to visit and sells apple cider and old-fashioned food products. Its entrance is located on East Spring Street which runs along the side of the park off Main Street. Be sure to also stop in Jenny's Ice Cream Shop next to the mill, with award-winning ice cream in the most unique flavors.

Akron Falls. Two waterfalls can be seen where Murder Creek drops over the Onondaga Escarpment in the Village of Akron. Both located in Akron Falls County Park, Lower Akron Falls is narrow and 50 feet high and Upper Akron Falls is curtain-like and 20 feet high. Both can dry up in mid-summer. Murder Creek was named for a murder that took place near it long ago.

The Upper Falls is unique in that it has an opening to an extensive cave at the bottom of and behind the falls. If you want to see it, you have to go when the falls is dry in mid-summer; in other words, the wrong time for waterfall touring. The cave is large and a mile

Upper Akron Falls (cave is behind the cascade)

or more in length, but its collapsing ceiling and confusing maze of passages make it very dangerous. That is why officials have installed a metal gate over the opening. Another cave opening has recently formed where the river pours through a sinkhole.

Indian Falls. Indian Falls is aptly named, since it is very near the Tonawanda Indian Reservation. It is created by the 20-foot drop of Tonawanda Creek, also appropriately named, since "Tonawanda" is Iroquois for "swift water." The 100-foot wide curtain cascade is located in the hamlet of Indian Falls, located south of the Iroquois National Wildlife Refuge (see Swallow Hollow entry). A historic plaque on a nearby road tells of the Great Sachem Chief, Donehogawa, who was born in 1828 in a log cabin overlooking Indian Falls. As he was known in English, Gen. Ely Samuel Parker became President Grant's military secretary and drafted the terms of the Confederacy's surrender at Appomattox in 1865. Later, he became the country's *first* Commissioner of Indian Affairs.

Morganville Falls. Located in the off-the-beaten-path picturesque village of Morganville just east of Batavia, this 27-foot high falls drops off a protruding ledge into a secluded, mossy amphitheatre. Not visible from roads, it is reached by a steep path down the ravine slope to Black Creek, a Genesee River tributary.

Buttermilk Falls at Leroy. This 60-foot high falls drops off an overhanging ledge that projects 20 feet out. The falls is especially impressive during heavy spring runoff, and as the photo shows, can look very much like a smaller-sized Niagara. The most common name for waterfalls is "Buttermilk" Falls. Since there are other Buttermilk Falls in Rochester, Hamilton, Westfield and Collins Center, the community associated with each falls is added to distinguish them. This falls is on Oatka Creek, a tributary of the Genesee River.

Honeoye Falls. How could a name for a falls be more romantic sounding than Honeoye (pronounced "honey-eye")? Unfortunately, the name comes from an Iroquois word for "finger-lying" which refers to an incident in which an Indian, bitten by a snake, cut his finger off. This 20-foot high falls is conveniently located in downtown Honeoye Falls village, which of course was named after the cascade. Like Glen Falls, its setting is enhanced by a bright-red old fashioned mill on the opposite bank. The creek is a tributary of the Genesee River.

It is fascinating to realize that all of the above waterfalls are tributaries of either the Niagara or Genesee Rivers, which means that the water that flows over each of these falls later drops *again* over Niagara Falls or Rochester's Genesee Falls. The best time to see the waterfalls is April through June when water flow is highest.

Devils Pulpit. A strange mushroom-shaped rock formation located along Rt. 5 between Batavia and Leroy. Like the waterfalls, the bedrock projection is made of Onondaga dolomite. Indian legend says that a giant got captured by a chief and was chained to the rock. In his attempt to escape, he ran around and around the rock till he wore the lower part away. Science's version is that natural erosion processes caused the lower part to flake off at a faster rate than the cap, leading to the bizarre shape. It is 8 feet high and 10 feet across.

The Birthplace of Jello. Why is this mentioned? Because I saw it marked on a brochure about Genesee County. "America's

Most Famous Dessert" was invented by Leroy resident Pearl Wait in 1897. Four years later, sales of "Jell-O" topped $250,000. As long as you're visiting Buttermilk Falls, you may as well stop by the historic Leroy House on 23 East Main St., Leroy (716) 768-7433) to see memorabilia about the jiggly dessert.

Directions:

To tour the Onondaga "necklace" of waterfalls, you can start from either the Buffalo end or the Rochester end.

To Start at the Buffalo Point of This Tour: From Ontario, take Queen Elizabeth Way to the bridge at either Niagara Falls or Lewiston, take Rt. 190 south to Rt. 290 east and exit at Main Street east. From points south and southwest, take the NY Thruway (Rt. 90) east to Exit 50 (Rt. 290/Niagara Falls) and leave Rt. 290 at Main Street east. From Buffalo, head up Main Street toward the village of Williamsville.

Once on Main Street in Williamsville, drive past the Town Hall, cross the bridge over Ellicott Creek and take the next left onto Mill Street. Take the first left onto Glen Avenue and park in the lot you will see on your right. Walk across the river bridge and turn left into the park. Upstream a short distance is the first falls of your tour, **Glen Falls**. Make sure to walk through the rest of the small but beautiful park. To visit the old mill and the ice cream shop, take the walkway upstream past the falls and turn right when you reach Main Street. Turn right at the next block.

To get to the next waterfall, continue east on Main Street (Rt. 5). When you reach Clarence Hollow, note that the hill that the car climbs up, and the vista to the left after you leave Clarence, is the Onondaga Escarpment. When you reach Rt. 93, turn left and drive 0.9 miles to Parkview Road, where you will see a sign for Akron Falls. Turn right. Take the next right again, which is is the park road (do not cross the bridge over the river). After 0.6 mile, turn left into a gravel parking lot; the trail is off the left side of the lot as you enter. **Lower Akron Falls** is a 1/8 mile walk.

To see **Upper Akron Falls**, start from the parking lot and walk upstream along the park road. At the park entrance gate, turn left onto Skyline Drive, then a left on State Street over the creek. When you've crossed the creek, *immediately* turn left across a grassy field and down a wide, grassy trail. A few hundred feet later, a narrow path to your left will take you to the Upper Falls. If the water is flowing well, you'll see a falls with a very different character from its companion just 600 feet downstream. If you go in midsummer, you'll get to see the gated cave opening. You'll also be able to walk across the dry creek bed to a spot on the opposite side just behind the dry falls crest and see the new sinkhole cave opening. Remember, the hole was once the cave ceiling -- that is why entering the cave is very dangerous!

To get to your fourth falls, drive to the above-described State Street, cross the bridge and turn right on East Avenue. East Avenue will come to a five-way intersection. Directly across the street from East Avenue is Knapp Road; just to the left of Knapp is Indian Falls Road, cutting off on a diagonal. Follow Indian Falls Road and it will change its name to Akron Road before reaching Rte. 77. Turn left on 77 and then immediately left again onto Gilmore Road *without crossing the creek*. Immediately on the right side of Gilmore is a tavern (ornately named Falconcrest Bar & Grill). Park in the lot and see **Indian Falls** next to the building. You can also view it from inside the tavern.

To see the historic marker, continue on Gilmore Road and make the first left onto Akron Road. The plaque is just ahead.

Proceed to your next treat by turning right (south) on Rte. 77 and then your first left onto Indian Falls Road. It will cross over the NY Thruway and end at Rte. 5. Turn left on Rte. 5 and pass through the city of Batavia. After you have left Batavia, you'll pass Seven Springs Road on your left and then Town Line Road on you right. 0.3 mile after Town Line Road, you will see a NY Department of Transportation building on your left. Turn into the driveway and park. The **Devils Pulpit** is to the left of the building a couple hundred feet away across a lawn next to a metal utility fence. You'll know you have driven passed it if you come to Prole Road.

For your next falls, continue east on Rte. 5 to Rte. 237 and turn left. After 1.4 miles, you will see Morganville Road to the left where 237 swings right. Turn onto Morganville Road and then take your first right (East Morganville Road). Drive only 0.1 mile to a bridge over a small creek. Pull into a dirt road *immediately* after the first house you pass on the left. **This is private property, so show your respect and leave it exactly as you found it!** Walk exactly 100 feet down the road, looking for a small path to your left. The path descends steeply into the ravine to the creek bottom, where you will see **Morganville Falls** to your left.

When you return to your car, turn left onto the road and will reach Rte. 237. Drive *across* 237 to Randall Road on the other side. When Randall Road reaches Rte. 19, drive *across* it to North Street Road. Drive 0.15 mile on North Street Road and, just as the road turns sharply to the right, park on your left at a gravel road next to a farm house. If you drive over the creek, you've gone too far.

Walk up the gravel road and it will quickly end at an abandoned railroad line corridor. Turn right, *walk only 50 feet,* and you will see a path down the embankment to your left. Follow the path parallel to the railroad corridor until it reaches the creek and **Buttermilk Falls. Take caution at the edge of the cliff.**

To get to the last falls, return to Rt. 19 and turn left into the village of Leroy (the **"Birthplace of Jello"**!). Turn left (east) on Rt. 5. When you reach the village of Avon, admire the beautiful homes, architecture and the village green. After Avon, turn left (north) on Rt. 15 (West Henrietta Road). Just *before* Rt. 15 crosses over Rt. 390, turn right onto Honeoye Falls Road. Take it over 390 and enter downtown Honeoye Falls, where you can see the last 'pearl' in the Onondaga 'necklace' of waterfalls, **Honeoye Falls.** It is behind Town Hall with convenient parking. A good frontal view can be seen from where East Avenue (one block ahead) crosses the river. In summer, it dries to a trickle.

To return, take Honeoye Falls Road back to Rt. 15 and turn right (north) to where it reaches the entrance to Rt. 390. Take 390 north and then exit to NY Thruway west to Buffalo. Take note of the highway mile markers. At Mile 387 just before the Batavia Exit 47, you will drive between cliffs of the Onondaga Escarpment.

To Start at the Rochester Point of This Tour: From Rochester area, take Rt. 31 to Pittsford and turn onto Rt. 65 south toward Mendon Ponds Park. It will cross the Thruway and soon enter downtown **Honeoye Falls** village where you can see the falls of the same name.

Then return to Rt. 65 and head south, turn left (west) on Rt. 5 & 20, cross Rt. 390 and pass through Avon. Stay on Rt. 5 to Leroy (the 'Birthplace of Jello'!), where you turn right on Rt. 19. Turn right on North Street Road. Now follow the directions given previously for **Buttermilk Falls.**

After seeing Buttermilk Falls, return to Rt. 19 and cross it onto Randall Road. Take Randall Road *across the railroad tracks* until it ends at Rt. 237. Cross 237 to East Morganville Road and slowly drive to where it crosses a creek. Then turn around, cross back over the creek, pass the first house on your left and pull into a dirt road on your left just after that.house. Follow the directions previously given to walk to **Morganville Falls.**

After seeing this falls, return to Rt. 237 and take it south to Rt. 5. Turn right (west) and 0.5 mile after Prole Road on your right, pull into the NY Department of Transportation building driveway. Follow directions given previously for **Devils Pulpit**.

Continue west on Rt. 5 through Batavia. Turn right (north) on Rt. 77, which will cross the Thruway and then reach a sign for Indian Falls hamlet (do not follow signs for Indian Falls *Lake*). When you reach the bridge over the river (don't cross it), turn left on Gilmore Road. Follow earlier directions to **Indian Falls**.

Where Gilmore Road meets Akron Road, turn right (west) and take it to the village of Akron where it meets the intersection of Scotland, East, Knapp and Crittenden roads. Continue straight ahead onto East Avenue and take the next left onto State Street. Cross the creek, and turn right onto Skyline Road till it reaches the entrance to Akron Falls Park. Drive 0.3 mile and park on the right in the gravel lot next to the nature trail. Follow directions previously given for **Akron Falls**.

After seeing both Upper and Lower Akron Falls, continue through the park to the western gate and drive to Rt. 93 south to Rt. 5-Main Street. Turn right on Rt. 5, cross Rt. 78 and continue into the village of Williamsville. Turn right onto Mill Street and follow the previously given directions to **Glen Falls**.

To return home via the NY Thruway, return east on Rt. 5. Turn right on Rt. 78 and it will reach the entrance to the Thruway. Note that at the Thruway's Mile Post # 388, you will pass between cliffs of the Onondaga Escarpment.

Buttermilk Falls at Leroy

THE BIZARRE BADLANDS OF NEW YORK STATE

An unforgettable tour of a sculptured fantasy of rock chimneys, spires, dragon backs, knife-edge ridges, vistas and odd rock formations overlooking a wild shore of Lake Ontario.

Distance: 1.8 miles round trip

Difficulty: Moderate

Notable Features:

Chimney Bluff: Located in an unpublicized, undeveloped state park, this weird area looks like a piece of the Dakota Badlands transplanted along Lake Ontario. It is a photographer's, child's and sightseer's paradise with 250-foot cliffs, intricately and strangely carved rock formations towering over the lake. **One of the scenic highlights of the entire Northeast U.S.!**

Chimney Bluff was formed by the Ice Age glaciers. The glaciers deposited an elongated hill of compacted gravel, called a drumlin. When the glaciers melted away, Lake Ontario's waters rose and reached the level of the glacial drumlin. The lake's waters battered the hill during storms, eroding parts of it away, and rains caused parts of the hill to slide into the lake. The erosion led to the bizarre forms we see today.

There are about nine badland ridges, with names like Drunkard's Leap, Disappearing Point and Stonehenge Point. Among the odd rock formations are the Dragon's Back, The Dragon's Horn, and Castle Spires. Some of the knife-edge ridges are indeed like knife edges; they are as narrow as 2 inches wide and up to 100 feet high!

Best time to visit is May through October. In the spring, the forest wildflowers are fantastic. In the summer, the lake breeze and waves are refreshing. In the autumn, the fall colors make the rock scenery even more amazing. Avoid heavy rain periods which will make your hike very, very muddy. Winter lake ice lasts into April and can make the shore impassable.

An unusual option: do a hike on a night forecast to be cloudless and with a full moon. The rock formations will be eerie, surreal and even more unforgettable. Do a night hike after having supper at the beach!

Cautions: Some of the trails are very close to the edge of high cliffs or thread along high promontories. Don't make this the last scenic wonder you see!

Poison ivy grows at certain points along the trail in the middle section of the bluff. It often dangles over the trail. Don't be paranoid, just learn to recognize it and maneuver around it. It won't grab you, and you can only get it if you touch it. Only a portion of people get a rash from it, anyway.

Take photos of some of the most distinctive sculptured forms. When you go back in future years, you will be able to see how rapidly they change. One stunning 15-foot tall feature, "Hitchhiker's Thumb," was only a knob when I returned two years later! New forms are created every year.

Directions:

From Buffalo and points west and south, take NY Thruway (Rt. 90) east. From Rochester, take Rt. 490 *east* to the NY Thruway. Thirty miles east of Rochester, get off at Exit 42 (Lyons - Rt.14). From Syracuse and points east, take the the NY Thruway *west* to Exit 42.

From Exit 42, head north on Rt. 14 toward the Village of Lyons. Continue through town, cross Rt. 104 and, half mile later, enter the tiny village of Alton. Turn right (east) on Old Ridge Road. Cross the mouth of Sodus Bay, an arm of Lake Ontario.

At the first 4-way intersection after Sodus Bay, turn left onto Lake Bluff Road. About 1.7 miles later, turn right onto Lummisville Road. After 0.75 miles, make a left at the next road, East Bay Road. Exactly two miles later, you'll pass a road on you right (Slacht Road), then a wetland area and *you will bear right at the next fork* (staying on East Bay Road). One mile later, you will "hit" Lake Ontario. A steep wooded bluff will be to your left, with an entrance to a crude dirt parking lot. Park here.

(You will know if you did not continue on East Bay Road if you do not see the lake after driving a while on what is called Garner Road. Turn around and look for a sharp left to get back onto East Bay Road north.)

From the parking lot, walk straight to the lake edge and climb

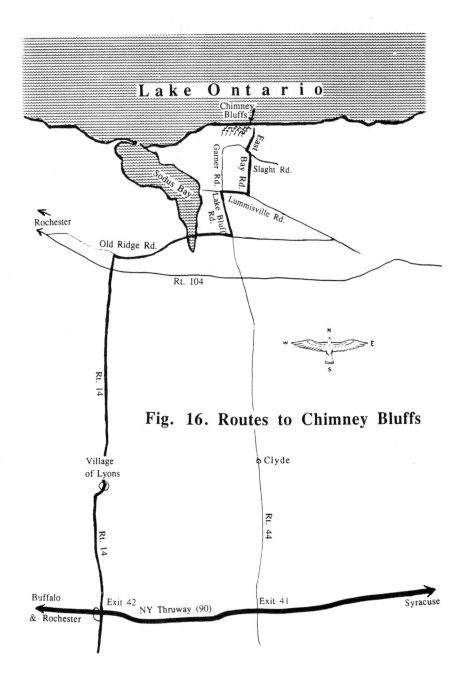

Fig. 16. Routes to Chimney Bluffs

Fig. 17. Chimney Bluffs

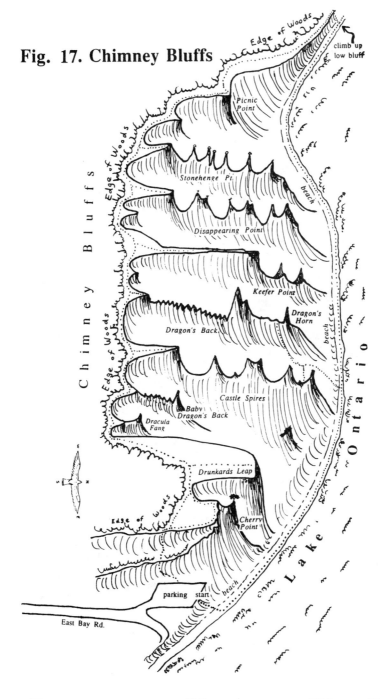

down the steep bank to the cobble beach along Lake Ontario. Turn left toward the high bluffs. You will soon come to the remarkable rock formations. As you pass each one, make sure to climb into the gullies between the ridges and up the sides of the more accessible ones, which will appear totally different than from below. Try to climb to the top of a knife-edge ridge. Each little valley is a different display of forms.

The beach trail will finally pass all the badland ridges. When the bluff along the shore lowers and gets very close to the cobble beach, start watching for a route up the bluff. Soon, the bluff will be only 10 feet above the beach. Scurry up the first accessible point.

At the top of the low bluff, turn left and follow the edge upward as the bluff rises higher and higher. You will soon reach Picnic Point and the first panorama above the badland formations. This is a perfect place to eat lunch. Follow the bluff edge, stopping to admire the vista, and climb to the end of each promontory, which bears a colorful name reflecting its appearance or what happened there. Keefer Point was named for a Labrador retriever who slipped off the cliff, fell vertically 100 feet, and to everyones' astonishment, got up, climbed up the gully to the top, and sat down without a scratch!

For the more adventurous, climb onto the Dragon's Back (note there is also a "Baby's Dragon's Back" a little further ahead for little kids). See how far you can walk or crawl on the saw-toothed, narrow ridge. The gravelly slope may look steep and intimidating, but it's not dangerous.

After walking past nine lines of ridges, the path comes to a downward slope into forest. Follow it steeply down into the woods and you will reach the parking lot and your car.

Climbing the Dragon's Back at Chimney Bluffs

THE SACRED PLACE WHERE THE IROQUOIS NATION WAS BORN, GANONDAGAN

A gentle walk through a place of powerful vibrations where the Iroquois Confederacy was born in peace, and where a European army destroyed its capital in war. Trails loop through this National Historic Site across scenic hilltops offering vistas, with dozens of signs vividly depicting what happened there. One woodland trail points out each of the important plants and trees used by the Seneca for food, medicine and other uses.

Distance: Three separate trails, two short and one moderately longer, totalling 3 miles in all..

Level of Difficulty: Easy.

Notable Features:

Ganondagan State Historic Site: A state park south of Rochester where one can step back 300 years and re-live the stirring and tragic events that make this place so important to Native people and helped shape the new American nation that was born a century later. The powerful human events and the peaceful beauty of the place evoke a feeling of reverence as you walk over breezy hilltop meadows and through hushed woodlands filled with bird song and wildflowers. In fact, the vibrations of this place led to its being listed in the book *Sacred Sites: A Traveler's Guide to North America's Most Powerful, Mystical Landmarks* (by Natasha Peterson, 1988, Contemporary Books).

The Iroquois nations do not need a book description of this site, since it is the place where their confederacy was born long ago. A man named the Peacemaker taught a powerful philosophy called the Great Law of Peace and succeeded in uniting five tribal nations into one confederacy that spanned most of New York State. His vision was a predecessor to the idea of a "United Nations" dedicated to justice and peace and based on the principle that disputes can be settled by ration and negotiations. Other Iroquois principles that Western Society later adopted were that leaders were servants of the people; citizen participation in government; female suffrage; and non-violent impeachment of officials.

While no "secret" to Native People, history buffs and some area residents, Ganondagan (pronounced gan-ON-duh-gan) was

Fig. 18. Ganondagan, Iroquois Nation Birthplace

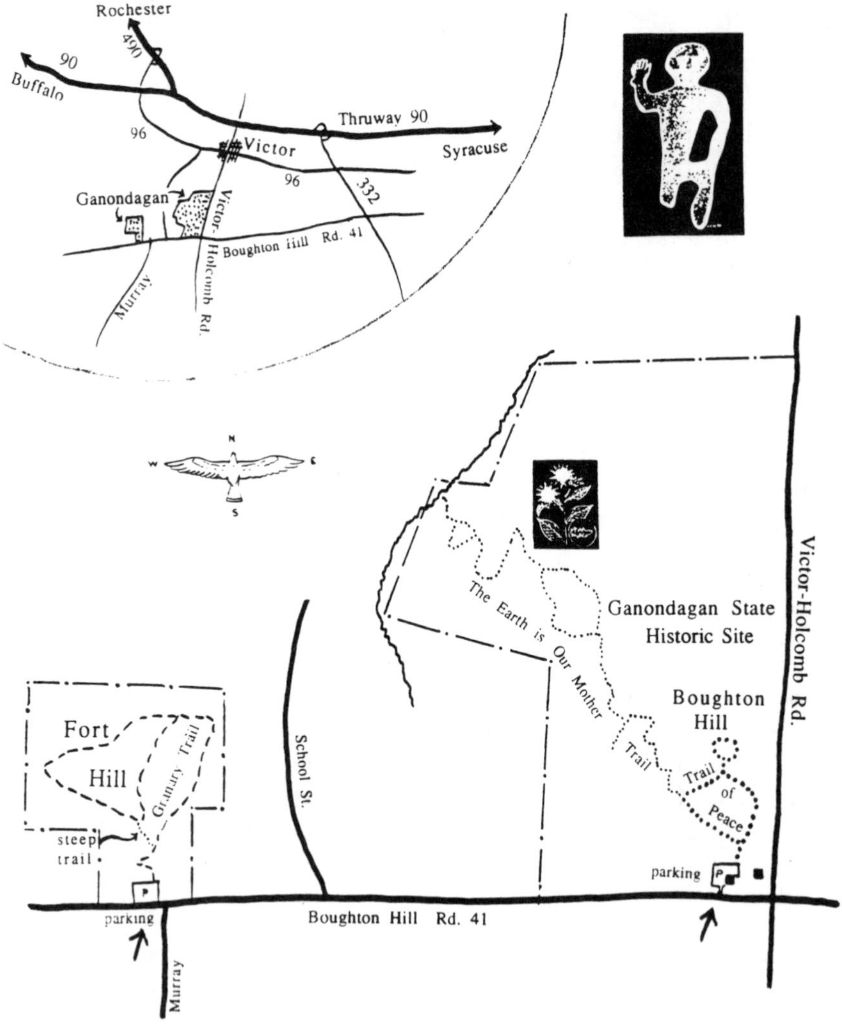

chosen as a "Secret Places" entry because it is poorly known by most people, and the Native contribution to democracy is under-appreciated.

The State Historic Park has a small museum and fascinating video on the site, and offers scheduled events such as Native story tellers and craftsmen, dance powwows and traditional song festivals, stargazing and other workshops.

Boughton Hill and the Trail of Peace. This 0.35 mile long trail forms a figure-8 across a broad hilltop meadow where once stood the great longhouse, village, burial places and livestock surrounded by wood fortifications. This was one of the Iroquois capitals. The story of the Great Law of Peace and the birth of the Confederacy is told along the trail. Also told is the account of the terrible destruction by the French army. In summer, the trail passes milkweed heavy with honey-scented blossoms, fragrant wild rose, and bobolinks and other birds trilling their melodies.

The Earth is Our Mother Trail. This is the only "ethno-botanical" trail I have ever seen. Along its one-mile length (2 mi. round trip), it describes many of the plants central to Seneca culture. The cultivated staples are "the Three Sisters," corn, squash and beans. Artistically inscribed plaques located next to many wild plants describe the Seneca uses for them. Examples are cattail, white pine, sugar maple, hickory, spicebush, and basswood. The trail takes you through quiet woods and thickets and ends at a creek with a small, pretty cascade.

Fort Hill and the Granary Trail. Separated from the main section of the park is Fort Hill, 0.8 mile to the west. Atop this prominent 30-acre mesa was a fort protected by a palisades of 13 foot-long oak logs a half mile around. It protected the largest granary, or corn storage facility, of the Seneca. The trail winds around Fort Hill through woods and then ascends to the meadow-covered summit, which offers sweeping views of the surrounding rolling hills and farmland. Plaques give a blow-by-blow account of the French attack on the fort, using the words of 17th century writers.

The Senecas were caught in the age-old conflict between the British and the French. After establishing a thriving fur trade with the French, they expanded their trade with the British. This infuriated the French so they decided to annihilate the Senecas and amassed their army to attack.

Unfortunately, the warriors were away in another territory, leaving the village and the fort defenseless. After a counter-ambush failed, the inhabitants fled. On July 15, 1687, the French, disappointed to find the village and fort empty, destroyed every thing in sight, including about a *million* bushels of corn that had been grown and harvested to feed the entire region.

Although the French destroyed the Seneca trade center, they did not destroy their culture. Instead, they simply made enemies of the Seneca, which benefited the British by strengthening their foothold in the "New World." In the end, ironically, the French lost the struggle to dominate North America.

Ganondagan stands as a testament to the continuation of the Seneca people in spite of the forces that set out to destroy them. It also reminds us of the contribution Native peoples made in the shaping of America and its democratic tradition.

Directions:

From Rochester, take Rt. 490 east to the NY Thruway (Rt. 90) east. From Buffalo, Ontario and points west and southwest, go to the Thruway east. From Syracuse and points east, take Thruway west. From points south, take Rt. 390 north to the Thruway east.

From Exit 44, take Rt. 332 south to the second traffic light. Make a right on County Road 41, which becomes Boughton Hill Road. At the top of the hill where there is a caution light, cross the intersection and park in the second driveway on the right.

Obtain brochures and trail maps from the visitor center (open daily 9 to 5, mid-May through Labor Day; Wed. to Sun., 9 to 5 the rest of the year). Two trails start right from the visitor center.

To get from the main site to the Fort Hill site, turn right (west) out of the parking lot and drive 0.8 mile until you reach the grassy parking lot on your right, with Fort Hill rising behind it. The trail begins at the back end of the parking lot. Once you have seen everything at the top of hill, you can take a shortcut down the steep bluff of the hill. Find it between trailside plaques # 7 and 9.

For more information, call (716) 924-5848.

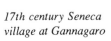

17th century Seneca village at Gannagaro

credit: John Fadden

VALENTINE FLATS: THE LITTLE PARADISE

A beautiful walk to a wild and secluded valley with terrific vistas, waterfalls, a unique natural pyramid hill, and a traditional skinny dipping beach.

Distance: 3-mile round trip

Level of Difficulty: Easy except for a short, steep scramble into the valley. Optional side trip up Pyramid Hill is strenuous but short.

Notable Features:

Zoar Valley Canyon: This is the steep valley cut by the Main and South Branches of Cattaraugus Creek, which forms the boundary between Erie and Cattaraugus Counties. The canyon is the second deepest in Western New York (415 feet deep) and is seven miles long in this section. Most of this section of the canyon is within State Forest, which means it is open to the public.
   The canyon is one of the two wildest areas in Western New York and is the wildest spot in Erie County. It contains 14 waterfalls!
   The Point: : An extremely narrow rock peninsula that juts into Zoar Valley Canyon, 120 feet above Cattaraugus Creek. Provides a wild and wonderful vista! When you reach the end of this sharp promontory, you can honestly say "I see the point!"
   Valentine Flats: A remarkable terrace or raised flat area perched *above* the Cattaraugus Creek, but *below* -- and completely surrounded by -- the cliffs of Zoar Valley Canyon. It is a delightful place to seek peace and solitude since it is inaccessible to motor vehicles. No sign of civilization can be seen or heard except an occasional airplane (which is often drowned out by the rushing noise of the river). Valentine Flats' 160 acres is a mixture of field, woods, walnut plantation and river shore. Raspberries and blackberries are abundant for the picking. It is truly a little paradise. During the Ice Age, the creek flowed through and cut this valley, but receded to the narrower channel you see today.
   Skinny Dipping Beach: Located at the edge of Valentine Flats where the South Branch meets the Main Cattaraugus Creek. This idyllic swimming and sunning area has been a traditional skinny dipping beach since the 1960s when hippies "liberated" the

area from the inhibitions of prudish society. On a hot summer Sunday, dozens of bathers gather here at this perfect place.

Pyramid Hill: A unique 120-foot high hill, shaped like a forest-covered three-sided pyramid. Because of the forest covering it, the distinct pyramid shape is not obvious from a distance. To see it, you must climb up the narrow ridge of the pyramid. The top is only 15-feet wide, with a 120-foot sheer cliff on one side, directly above the river. From here, you get a wonderful panorama and a distant glimpse of one waterfall when it is most visible during heavy flow in spring. Pyramid Hill is one of the only such hills in eastern North America. It was formed when the Ice Age glacier melted and sent massive amounts of water flowing through Zoar Valley. The raging waters carved a channel around the hill, shaping it further. Then the water level receded to what we see today, to the current channel, which has continued to carve that side deeper.

Skinny Dip Falls: This 120-foot cascade drops off the cliff 500 feet downstream from where South Branch meets Main Cattaraugus Creek. It is best seen when its flow is heavy until early June.

Barebutt Falls: This 80-foot cascade plunges in seven steps off the north wall of Zoar Valley canyon. Because of forest cover, it can only be seen up close, but it can be heard quite a distance away in spring and early summer. You must cross Cattaraugus Creek from Valentine Flats to reach it.

Directions:

From the Buffalo area, take Rt. 62 south to Gowanda. From Ontario or Rochester directions, the NY Thruway takes you to Rt. 62 from Exit 58 at Hamburg. From points south of Gowanda, Rt. 17 will take you to Rt. 62 north or Rt. 353 north, both of which take you to Gowanda.

Once in downtown Gowanda, where Rt. 62 crosses Cattaraugus Creek, turn east onto Water Street, which parallels the creek along its *south* bank. As you follow it, the same street will change names before becoming labelled Broadway where it veers right. It will suddenly ascend a steep hill. *Just at the top of the hill, watch carefully for Point Peter Rd. on your left!* Take scenic Point Peter Rd. until you reach tiny Valentine Flats Road on your left. Drive to its dead-end and park. **Make sure you are not obstructing the road or the private driveway at its end! If you do, you will get ticketed.**

Walk on the dirt road through its dead-end barrier. Follow the woods road 1/4 mile until you reach a small meadow in the woods. Bear left and follow the ever-narrowing trail to the end of **The Point** (also called Point Peter). The panorama is breathtaking! **Caution: it is dangerous to get too close to the edge.**

Return to the meadow. On the opposite end of the meadow is a woods road that has just been built. Follow it 500 feet until it ends. Continue on the thin trail that hugs the edge of the steep bank until it widens again and follow it down into the valley. If it fades out, walk with the steep slope always to your right until you reach the creek. At the creek, follow it downstream till it joins with the larger river.This is The Junction and **Skinny Dip Beach** where South Branch joins Main Cattaraugus Creek. Admire the high toothed cliffs above you, and the human scenery below you. Join in and take a dip! **Caution: the current in the Main Branch is treacherous in spring and medium to high flow periods in summer. Many people have drowned here.**

To get to Pyramid Hill, follow the river downstream using the trail along the top of the high bank. The trail will soon veer away from the creek and skirt the bottom of a steep wooded hill to your right. This is **Pyramid Hill**. Notice the fascinating tangle of huge grape vines on your left. Some of these may be over a century old. Right after the tangle of grape vines, you will notice a steep ridge up the wooded slope on your right. If you choose to climb to the dramatic vista on top of Pyramid Hill, climb the ridge where it reaches closest to the trail. After a steep climb of 50 feet, it will become a clear path over a backbone-like ridge right to the tiny summit. Brace yourself for an exhilarating view. It's also a secluded place to sun yourself in summer. Return by taking the same route down.

From the bottom of Pyramid Hill, you may wish to continue further on the trail. It will wind through a field filled with tall grass, shrubs, raspberry, blackberry and abundant wildflowers. The berry-picking in late July and August will add one more fond memory of your visit to this little paradise.

Many people explore the canyon by walking *up* either the Main Branch or the South Branch. These routes are depicted on the map and described in the other Zoar Valley "Secret Places" entries.

To visit **Skinny Dip Falls**, cross the South Branch (only in the summer during low water). Once on the opposite side, pass under the jutting, prominent cliff and onto the south shore of Main Branch. Follow it 500 feet upstream and then cut into the woods where an inconspicuous streamlet emerges. Follow the brook 200

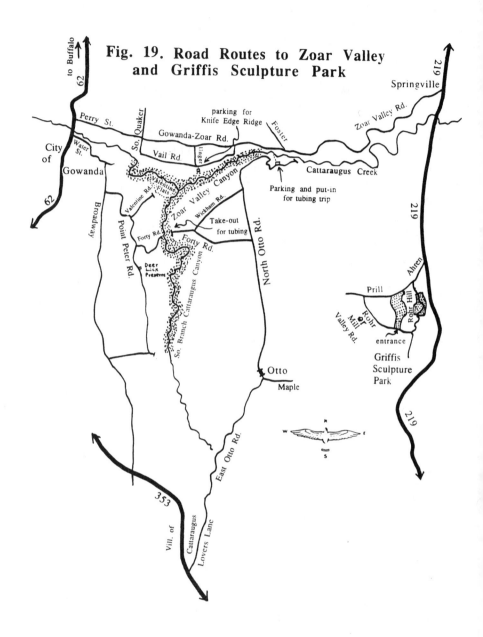

Fig. 19. Road Routes to Zoar Valley and Griffis Sculpture Park

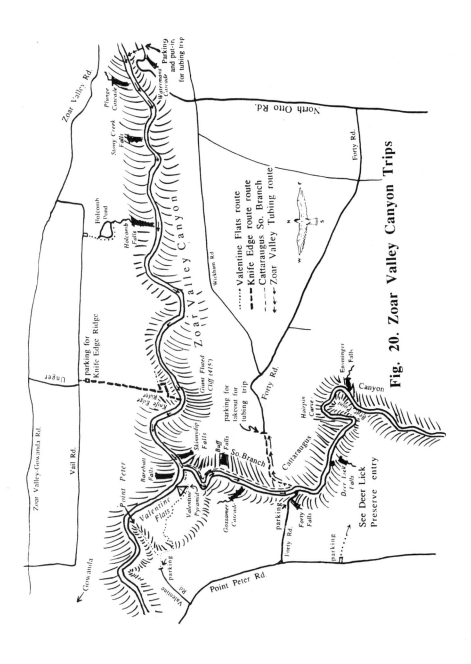

Fig. 20. Zoar Valley Canyon Trips

feet to Skinny Dip Falls for a real experience! The falls reduces to a trickle by midsummer.

To visit Barebutt Falls, wade the Main Branch Cattaraugus Creek 100 feet upstream from the Junction, where a line of boulders and rocks makes the stream shallow. **Don't dare try it except in the low flow season!** Once across, head straight into the woods for the canyon cliff 400 feet away. When you reach the cliff bottom, follow it to the left until you reach Barebutt Falls. You will see the lowest two cascade steps. You can only see the upper six steps of cascading water by ascending the very steep ravine slope.

Before you leave Valentine Flats, pick up any cans or litter left by less caring souls. This will help keep this beautiful place a "little paradise."

Return to Valentine Flats and back to your car on the same trail that you took in.

Note: You can combine this hike with the South Branch Cattaraugus hike.

Skinnydip Beach beneath towering cliffs in Valentine Flats

CANYON COUNTRY: CATTARAUGUS CREEK AND GOSSAMER CASCADE

Beautiful hike through a scenic, waterfall-lined canyon to a remote, wilderness retreat and skinnydipping beach.

Distance: 3.5 miles round trip

Level of Difficulty: Easy to moderate, except for the stretch where the river meets the bottom of the cliff and you may have to wade in the water.

Notable Features:

Zoar Valley Canyon
Skinny Dip Beach   See description under Valentine Flats Adventure

Skinny Dip Falls
Valentine Flats

South Branch Cattaraugus Creek Canyon: This creek cuts through an impressive 200 to 250-foot deep canyon until it meets the Main Branch Cattaraugus Creek at Valentine Flats. Eight waterfalls drop gracefully off its cliffs!

Forty Road Falls: This unique 75-foot falls plunges off a cliff right next to -- almost on top of -- a narrow auto bridge that descends into the 200-foot deep canyon. The falls then cascades under the bridge to the bottom. The bridge was almost torn away by the Great Flood of 1986, but it has just been rebuilt. It is the primary access into the valley for hikers.

Gossamer Cascade: An extraordinarily scenic cascade that appears as a 130-foot tall white ribbon. It drops off the west side of South Branch Cattaraugus.

Buff Falls: Another 120-foot cascade that plunges down the canyon wall. Although almost opposite Gossamer Cascade, it is not visible from the creek trail. A short side trail takes you through woods to its bottom.

Note: The hike all the way to Valentine Flats is only possible at low water (June through October) because high water floods out part of the route. Wear sneakers in summer so you can walk in the stream with better traction and speed and to avoid scraping your feet.

Caution: **Watch out for three-leaved poison ivy** along the first 1/2 mile or so of trail (in the woods only), starting from where Forty Road crosses the bridge over South Branch.

Directions:

To get to this "secret place," follow the directions to Valentine Flats given under that entry. Once you get to Valentine Road, continue another 0.7 miles south to Forty Road, which is the first left after Valentine Road. Note: as of this writing, Forty Road's sign was missing. You can either park at the top of the canyon or at the bottom. If you park at the top, you'll avoid the extremely steep drive down and the often-crowded parking situation at the bottom. Although there are 'no parking' signs in some places, at this time, cars are not being ticketed at the bottom or top if they are not obstructing the road or the private driveway at the top.

Where Forty Road descends steeply over the little bridge, stop to look at Forty Road Falls as it drops next to and then under the bridge. Then continue to the bottom of the valley. You can start your hike down the South Branch two ways. Just before the closed bridge over South Branch Cattaraugus Creek, there is trail to the left which takes you down to the creek. You can walk down the creek or cross it here to the other shore, which is

Ribbon-like Gossamer Falls

wider. Or you can cross the bridge over the creek to get to the woods trail on the other side. Although the bridge is closed to autos, the state has no objection to foot traffic across it, which requires climbing over the barriers. Immediately (40 feet) after crossing it, look carefully to your left for an inconspicuous and narrow trail over an embankment. Follow the path through the woods in a downstream direction.

After 1/4 mile, look for **Gossamer Cascade** on the opposite side -- make sure not to miss it! To see it better, you may wish to climb down to the river edge. Watch out for poison ivy.

After this point, back on the woods trail, start looking **carefully** for a little brook or flow of water coming in from the right bank (no more than several hundred feet past the view of Gossamer Cascade). Follow this trickling tributary into the woods. 400 feet of walking will take you to the bottom of **Buff Falls**. Return to the river again. Canyon walls will close in on the right, forcing you to either walk in the water or along a thread of a ledge at water's edge. After another sharp turn of the river, swimmin' holes will appear. But continue downstream to **Valentine Flats**. In summer, join the skinny dippers, walk to **Skinnydip Falls** and **Barebutt Falls**, and explore the rest of Valentine Flats (see Valentine Flats description).

Return home via the same route. An alternative is to combine the Valentine Flats hike and this hike. You can do this by using two cars, parking one at each end, or by hiking a longer distance to see all the features.

Sculpted cliffs off Knife Edge Ridge

KNIFE EDGE RIDGE AND GIANT
FLUTED CLIFF

Short hike across meadow and forest to spectacular bird's eye view atop the highest point over Zoar Valley Canyon and opposite one of the highest cliffs in New York, west of the Adirondacks.

Distance: 1.75 miles round trip

Difficulty: Easy to the top of the canyon. Strenuous if you descend the Knife Edge Ridge to the bottom of the canyon. Wear long pants to avoid being scratched by raspberry bushes along part of the route.

Notable Features:

Zoar Valley Canyon: See description under Valentine Flats Adventure

Knife Edge Ridge: A narrow, exposed shale ridge that provides an awesome view into the yawning gulf 400 feet below. It also provides a direct, though strenuous, route directly down into the deepest part of Zoar Valley Canyon. Lastly, it allows a view of Giant Fluted Cliff.

Giant Fluted Cliff: Second highest cliff in Western New York (after Letchworth Canyon's 550-foot cliff). The 415-foot cliff is fluted with regular indentations, hence its name. Because it faces due north, the sun never shines on it.

Directions:

From the directions of Rochester and Ontario, drive to the Buffalo area. From Buffalo, take Rt. 62 south to the outskirts of Gowanda. Turn left onto Perry Road. If you enter downtown Gowanda, you have gone too far. Perry Road turns into Gowanda-Zoar Rd. after it crosses railroad tracks. After driving 2.8 miles from Rt. 62, turn right onto Unger Rd, a little backwoods road. Take it until it ends at Vail Road. Turn left, drive only 50 feet (not further!) and turn right into a little gravel driveway which takes you to the dirt parking area for Zoar Valley State Multiple Use Area. If you drive past the large wooden "Zoar Valley Multiple Use Area" sign, you've passed it.

Follow the meadow trail at the end of the parking lot south until it reaches the woods at the other end of the large meadow, less than a half mile. Now you begin a short bushwhack. When the trail meets the forest edge, it turns left. Walk along the trail 200 feet further and you will see where three electric lines on poles cut through the woods. Turn right off the main trail and follow under the wires for 500 feet along an overgrown path through raspberry bushes. This may be a bit scratchy and prickly (wear long pants) but there is a hidden benefit if you go in late July: abundant raspberry picking. Fifty feet before you reach the last set of poles, head to the righthand side of the utility corridor to the margin of the woods. Continue thirty more feet toward the edge of the canyon, looking for a small trail inside the woods **which will parallel the edge of the gorge away from the electric lines**. Follow the little path through the forest; if it is sometimes hard to see, just always stay 5 to 25 feet from the canyon edge.

Walk roughly a half mile until you come to a large round boulder 20 feet from the edge, with an obstructed view across the canyon. Walk to the edge and you will see a bare ridge below you -- this is the **Knife Edge**. See the awesome vista of the yawning canyon and a tall, shaded cliff across the way. Admire the wildness, the virtual absence of human signs, the echoey roar of the creek. This is also a perfect picnic spot. Make sure to walk down onto the Knife Edge a ways to enhance the feeling of awe and wilderness.

If you wish to, continue down the ridge for a strenuous descent. The ridge broadens out and you end up scurrying down leafy slopes until you reach a forested terrace alongside the river. **Caution: Never descend this ridge except from mid-May until early October. Once the slope becomes icy, you will not be able to get back up!**

When you reach the bottom, enjoy the cool, mature forest. In May, the wild leeks, a kind of large gourmet onion, are abundant for the picking. Always leave a portion of the leek colony untouched. From the river's edge, peer up at **Giant Fluted Cliff**, on the opposite shore. In spring, whitewater rafters, kayakers and canoers shoot down the Cattaraugus rapids by the dozens. They have their own thrill, but they usually don't stop to appreciate the height of the cliff or to savor the wild leek. You can also have a rock throwing contest to see who can hit the cliff on the other side from the shore. Only two of us could reach it, and barely at that.

Return the same way you came. If you do it on a hot summer day, you better have a cool supply of water waiting for you!

TUBING ADVENTURE THROUGH
ZOAR VALLEY CANYON

A helluva roller coaster ride down the Cattaraugus Creek Canyon, past stunning waterfalls, towering cliffs, skinny dipping beach and wilderness.

Distance: 4.5 mile tubing trip down the river, and 1.5 mile walk back to the car.

Difficulty: The tubing part is easy, though paddling a tube through slow stretches can become rather tiring. Carrying the tubes back on the trail to the car is the tiring part.

    This route may also be canoed or kayaked if you are experienced. Note that dragging or carrying the canoe up the South Branch and steep Forty Road could be difficult.

Notable Features:

Zoar Valley Canyon:
Knife Edge Ridge:
Fluted Cliff:
Valentine Flats:
Skinny Dip Falls:
Skinny Dip Beach:
Barebutt Falls:
Pyramid Hill:
South Branch Cattaraugus Creek:
Buff Falls:
Gossamer Cascade:
Forty Road Falls:

} See Descriptions in preceding hikes

Zoar Valley Canyon Waterfalls: This voyage takes you past up to nine waterfalls! Besides the ones listed above, you will also be able to see:

    Waterman's Cascade (70 feet) - Extremely graceful cascade, easily visible from where the road descends after its steep curving route to the valley, only a short distance from where you parked.

    Plunge Cascade (80 feet) - the first cascade you can tube to. It is set back in the woods, not visible from the river.

Stoney Creek Falls (80 feet) - the most dramatic falls in Zoar Canyon. It plunges off a cliff almost directly into Cattaraugus Creek. The sight of it from your tube as you come around the bend is unforgettable.

Holcomb Falls (80 feet) - this waterfall drops through the woods. Its source is Holcomb Pond, accessible by trail from Vail Road.

The best time for inner tubing is during medium flow, typically during June. At this time, the water and air are warm enough for comfort, and the water is high enough to provide a thrill, but not rough enough to require life insurance policies. If it has been a dry spring, the water can get too low and the trip will provide no whitewater. You may even have to walk your tube through rocky areas. Remember, however, you are in the Zoar Valley Canyon to experience its beauty, not solely the thrill of its whitewater. In other words, you can't lose when you enter such a beautiful place.

Caution: Always wear a life jacket at all times! Do not do a tubing trip during spring high water season, March to early June. The water is too cold and Cattaraugus' whitewater is too dangerous in an inner tube. Only expert canoeists (or kayakers) should do it on their own at this time. You may instead choose one of the commercial, professionally-run rafting trips offered from Gowanda. Two whitewater rafting companies I know of are Adventure Calls, 20 Ellicott Ave., Batavia, NY 14020, (716) 343-4710, and Zoar Valley Rafting, P.O. Box 695, Dunkirk, NY 14048, (716)366-0205.

Instructions:
Equipment needed:
Two cars, one to park at the put-in spot, one to park at the take-out spot
Inner tubes (or small inflatable rafts)
Life jackets
Waterproof bag or a tethered float to hold lunches
Cords to pull tubes and lash food bags onto tubes or canoes
Sneakers
Wear short-sleeve shirts over your bathing suit if you go tubing. It will prevent the irritation caused by friction from paddling. It will also prevent you from burning to a crisp due to sunburn under the summer solstice.

Bring NO glass!
Leave NO garbage. Pack it in -- pack it out!

Directions:

Take two cars.

From Buffalo, Ontario or Rochester areas: Follow the directions to Gowanda and Broadway via Rt. 62, as described under the Valentine Flats entry. Do not leave Broadway, however. Follow it all the way south to Rt. 353. At 353, turn left (south). In the Village of Cattaraugus, turn left onto Lovers Lane Road.

Start your odometer. Lovers Lane's name may change to East Otto Road and it will lead you into the village of Otto. Watch carefully for North Otto Road on your left (at the 4-mile mark), which starts at a narrow bridge over a creek. Drive on North Otto Road to the junction of Forty Road. Turn left and drive to its end, which is at a gate and turn-around parking lot (the barricaded part of the road descends sharply down into South Branch Cattaraugus Creek valley). This is the take-out spot. Leave one car here, but take the car with the tubes to the put-in spot. This second car should be driven back along Forty Road (east) to North Otto Road. Turn left and drive 1.3 miles past the junction with Wickham and Bobseine Roads.

As you descend a steep and winding section, watch on your right for **Waterman's Cascade**. Park in the field/parking lot opposite the rustic entrance gate of a girl scout camp. This site is state-owned as a public put-in spot. Drag your stuff on the foot trail down to the river and begin your adventure.

From Jamestown, Olean or Pennsylvania directions: From Jamestown and points west, take Rt.17 east to Exit 16 - Randolph, take Rt. 242 to Little Valley and turn left on Rt. 353. From Olean and points east, take Rt. 17 west to Exit 20 - Salamanca and take Rt. 353 north. From Pennsylvania, take either Rt. 62 north to Rt. 17 and head east to Exit 16, or Rt. 219 north to Rt. 17 west to Exit 20 (see Jamestown or Olean directions for what's next).

From all these directions, once on Rt. 353, take it to the Village of Cattaraugus and turn right on Lovers Lane Road. From there, follow the directions given in the above paragraph which begins "Start your odometer."

Directions for River Tubing: The first two miles are placid water, with waterfalls located off tiny tributaries. Look carefully for seeps or small brooks entering the river from your right. Take out at these spots and follow the brooks into the woods to where they drop off as **Plunge** and **Holcomb Cascades**. You can't miss **Stoney Creek Falls**! Notice how it drops through the air, then cascades like drapery down a shale-layered rock apron.

The lower two miles close in with high cliffs. This is where the exciting rapids are. The biggest rapid is at the bottom of Fluted Cliff. Be sure to pull out after this big wave and admire the **Giant Fluted Cliff** (see Knife Edge description). You may want to also climb up **Knife Edge Ridge** for the spectacular view. After the sweaty climb, you'll appreciate returning to the cooling water.

The tube trip ends at the junction with South Branch Cattaraugus Creek, which enters from the left, just after an exciting rapids, and a high jutting cliff on the left.

Pull out as close to the South Branch inlet as possible. If you float past it, you enter the faster, larger stream which could carry you further than you prefer. Once out of the water, you are now in **Valentine Flats**, with its incredible secluded wilderness valley, swimmin' hole and skinny dipping area. Enjoy thyself!

To return, walk up the South Branch channel. You will have to carry your deflated tubes up the shallow, rocky stream. The instructions for this route are described under South Branch Cattaraugus Hike. Remember to enjoy the waterfalls along the way and watch for poison ivy. When you arrive at the little bridge over the South Branch, walk up the *left* bank to the abandoned part of Forty Road. It will lead steeply up to where your car is parked.

To drive back to pick up the first car, take Forty Road to North Otto Road, turn left and drive to reach the first car.

Deep in Zoar Valley Canyon

DEER LICK PRESERVE AND THE HAIRPIN CURVE

An extremely scenic hike through a Nature Conservancy preserve comprising a pristine segment of Zoar Valley, including a wild, hair-pin curved canyon, four waterfalls and a panorama.

Distance: 3.2 to 5.6 miles, depending on choice of route

Level of Difficulty: Easy to moderate to Bear Point; strenuous if you descend to the canyon bottom.

Notable Features:

> *Zoar Valley Canyon*   ⎫ See description under
>   ⎬   Valentine Flats
> *South Branch Cattaraugus* ⎭   Adventure

Deer Lick Preserve: A 630-acre forested nature preserve abutting Zoar Valley State Forest and upstream from the other Zoar Valley adventures described in this book. Deer Lick was designated by the U.S. Congress as a National Natural Landmark because of its ecological significance. It is a wild and beautiful place with a well-marked, extensive trail system.

Bear Point: Vista from a knife-edge ridge that is between the Hair Pin Curve of South Branch Cattaraugus Creek.

Hair Pin Curve: A 400-foot deep, remarkably curved canyon, wild and seldom visited, that almost loops back into itself.

Deer Lick Falls: A 70-foot falls that flow like drapery down the cliff from Deer Lick Preserve to the bottom of Zoar Valley Canyon. While the Preserve is named for the falls, it cannot be seen from the preserve's trail system. Instead, it must be seen by descending to the bottom of the canyon, below most of the preserve, or by walking through the creek bottom from Forty Road, downstream.

Actually, there are two other Deer Lick Falls. The Lower Falls drops six feet right into the Cattaraugus. The Upper Falls is situated upstream from the main Deer Lick Falls, inside the deep ravine. It drops 10 feet and is difficult to reach or see.

Directions:

Follow directions to Valentine Flats Road given in the Valentine Flats description. Instead of turning onto Valentine Flats

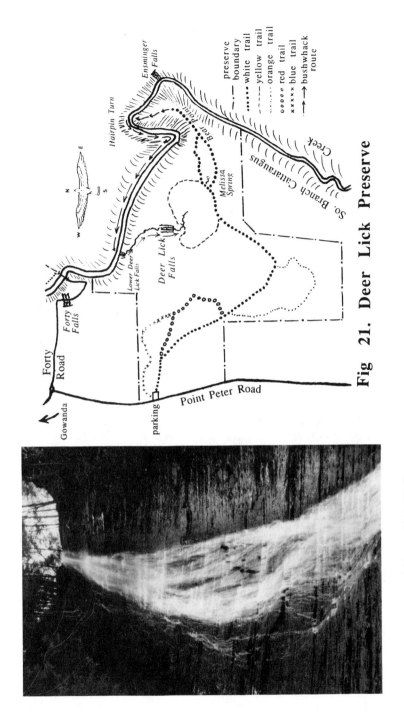

Fig 21. Deer Lick Preserve

preserve boundary
white trail
yellow trail
orange trail
red trail
blue trail
bushwhack route

Ensminger Falls

Hairpin Turn

So. Branch Cattaraugus Creek

Melissa Spring

Lower Deer Lick Falls

Deer Lick Falls

Bear Run

Forty Falls

Forty Road

Gowanda

Point Peter Road

parking

The water veil of Deer Lick Falls

Road, continue south 1.4 mile on Point Peter Road, looking on your left for "Deer Lick Preserve" sign. Park your car in the little lot.

Before you start, make sure you have a map of the preserve given in this book. You are entering a wild area. Take the white trail through mature maple and hemlock forest and enjoy the pure water a Melissa Spring (place hand over the lower end of the short vertical pipe, hold until water flows through the top of the pipe, then drink from the top). The trail leads to **Bear Point** (3.2 miles). Walk out on the point and enjoy the vista into the **Hair Pin Curve** of South Branch Cattaraugus Canyon.

From this point, you have two options. You can choose the adventure route down into the Hair Pin Curve, down the canyon to Deer Lick Falls, and up the falls back to the main trail. Or you can avoid the steep, trail-less climbing and return pretty much the way you came.

If you choose the adventure route, follow Bear Point's ridge (no trail) all the way down until it broadens out and descends to river bottom. At low water, you can explore the Hair Pin Curve of the remarkable gorge, upstream or downstream. If you head upstream 1/4 mile, you get to see 140-foot **Ensminger Falls** (see map), which flows well only in spring to early July.

If you head downstream, walk 3/4 mile and look for a small flow or seepage of water from the left bank. The six-foot high **Lower Deer Lick Falls** cascades over the bank there. Follow this brook into the woods until you reach 70-foot high **Deer Lick Falls**. For those of you experienced in climbing rocky slopes, carefully climb hand-over-hand along the side of the falls to the top. **Caution: this is only for experienced people. The rocks can be dangerously slippery!** Once at the top, enter the cool, shaded ravine and walk to **Upper Deer Lick Cascade**. Climb past it and just a little further up the winding ravine, you will link up with the yellow trail. *Look carefully for the trail where it crosses the brook -- you do not want to miss it!* Turn right on the trail and will take you to the white trail. Turn right on that and it will take you back to your car.

If you chose the easier option, you may wish to vary your return route by taking one or two of the loop trails (yellow, orange, red or blue) shown on your map.

SURREAL GRIFFIS SCULPTURE PARK

A surreal stroll through hilltop fields and vistas and past 100 bizarre, beautiful and bewitching statues and sculptures. One of the most unique and weird walks imaginable!

Distance: 0.5 to 4 miles, depending upon inclination.

Level of Difficulty: Easy in some sections, moderate in hilly and wooded sections.

Notable Features:

Griffis Sculpture Park: 400-acre park opened in 1967 that displays a remarkable collection of 100 giant metal figures and sculptures on open hillsides, in forests and around ponds. The park is in three sections. The largest is entered from Mill Valley Road and has a maze of trails to about 100 statues and creatures. The second section is reached by Rohr Hill Road and is in a meadow, although some statues and trails lie inside the forest at the field edge. The newest section is off Prill Road.
The types of statues include:

> Giant Amazon nude women, up to 15 feet tall
> Giant insects, mosquitoes, beetles, scorpions
> Giant animals, dinosaurs, birds, snail
> Kings, queens, dancing ladies, priests, busts
> A castle tower and a lighthouse you can climb up
> Weird arches, columns, mushrooms, a maze
> Submarine and pregnant "ladies" you can climb into
> Undefinable shapes and alien entities

In the main section off Mill Valley* Road, graceful sculpted women share a pond with a flock of equally graceful white swans (the warm-blooded kind!). There is also a small refreshment table, open in mild weather only. *also called Rohr Rd.

Directions:
From Buffalo, Rochester and Ontario, take NY Thruway (Rt.90) south to Rt. 219. Take 219 south into Springville. Continue on, cross the bridge over Cattaraugus Creek into Cattaraugus County. Five miles or so later, enter the hamlet of Ashford Hollow.

Ride a dinosaur at Griffis Sclupture Park!

Climb an Amazon Woman, too!

From the south, Rt. 17 connects with Rt. 219 north, which will also take you to Ashford Hollow. Ashford Hollow is 10.5 miles north of Ellicottville.

Once in Ashford Hollow, turn onto Ahrens Road, a small country road on your right when coming from the north. Make the first left off Ahrens Road onto Rohr Hill Road, a gravel road up a hill. **Note: this road is not plowed in winter and is hazardous when icy.** You will pass through the high meadow section of the park, but don't stop yet. Continue on Rohr Hill Road down a steep winding road to the bottom of the hill. Take a right onto Mill Valley Road and drive 1/2 mile. Immediately after passing little Mason Hill Road on your left, enter the park entrance and drive to the dirt parking lot. Allow a half day and lunch for this section. Then drive back to the Rohr Hill Road meadow section and allow two hours, in that order. Otherwise, you will miss the best stuff first. If you still have time and energy, visit the newest section, reached by driving north along Rohr Hill Road to where it meets Ahrens Road and turn left onto Prill Road.

For the more adventurous, linger at the Rohr Valley Road meadow section at sunset. Wander among and climb onto the various sculptures in the twilight and darkness, using a flashlight if desired. The darkness of a night excursion magnifies the surreal setting even more, making it a night you will remember for a long time.

What makes this site even more unique is that there is no admission charge! Therefore, it is worthwhile to support the Ashford Hollow Foundation for the Visual and Performing Arts, 30 Essex St, Buffalo, NY 14213 (716) 886-3616 or 67-A Mill Valley Road, East Otto, NY 14729, (716) 257-9344. The Buffalo facility has artist studios and a gallery. The foundation maintains the Sculpture Park grounds and trails and offers musical performances at the Sculpture Park's outdoor stage.

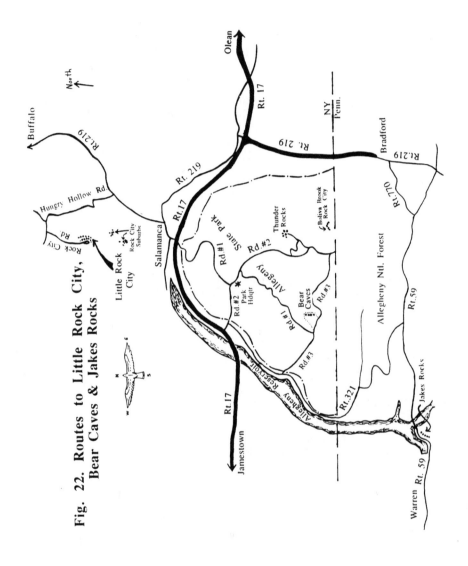

Fig. 22. Routes to Little Rock City, Bear Caves & Jakes Rocks

LITTLE ROCK CITY EXPLORATION

A seemingly unending labyrinth of odd blocks of colossal rocks, lined up like buildings on a forest hilltop, with little caves, "streets," "alleyways," "courtyards" and crevices to explore.

Distance: Total walk through and between Rock City "buildings" is one mile.

Level of Difficulty: Easy, except at a few spots where the surface of some "streets" is muddy, or where scurrying over rocks or through crevices is required.

Notable Features:

Little Rock City: Rock cities are unique rock formations composed of giant rectangular or sculpted boulders, often arranged in rows, forming fantasy "streets," "alleyways," and "buildings," sometimes interlaced with deep crevices and grottos. There are 29 rock cities in the region, but only 9 are open to the public.

Little Rock City is the largest rock city (50 acres) on publicly-owned land. It is located on McCarthy Hill within Rock City State Forest (2905 acres).

Some of its features include:

"*Broadway*" and "*Wall Street*" are the two longest "streets" or continuous rock-lined corridors. They are each 0.2 mile long. A shorter one is *Dark Alley*.

Several boulder and crevice caves and shelters are fun to crawl into with flashlights, such as the *Big and Little Subway, Slab Shelter, Courtyard Shelter* and *Leaning Rocks Shelter*.

Historic rock carvings are preserved under *Inscription Grotto*. Some date back to the 1800s and are fun to decipher.

The Courtyard and *Rockefeller Plaza* are two natural courtyards surrounded by a ring of humungus building-like boulders.

There are several "suburbs." The closest is *Slab City*, shown on the map. *Little Stone City* is located on another ridge about 1/2 mile south, not connected by trail.

A narrow "street" of Little Rock City

Other curiosities are *Birch Root Ladders*, a *Tree Bridge* and a *Stilt Tree*, and the *Abstract Gallery Wall* with curious rock patterns called boxwork.

You must bring boots, since some "streets" are muddy, even in summer, the driest time to visit. October provides stunning autumn colors!

Show your respect for nature by bringing a plastic bag to carry out cans and litter that less caring souls have dropped.

Other Rock Cities: Each of the region's rock cities is spectacular or unique in its own way and each is worth visiting. Most are on private land and are not accessible to the public. Besides Little Rock City, Jakes Rocks and Bear Caves (all described in this book), the publicly accessible ones are Thunder Rocks and Boliva Brook Rock City (Allegany State Park); Olean's Big Rock City; Panama Rock City; Alva Hill Rock City in Alva Hill State Forest, Allegany County; rock cities in Minister Valley Scenic Area, Allegheny National Forest; and the amazing Nelson-Kennedy Ledges State Park north of Youngstown, Ohio.

The privately-owned Big Rock City south of Olean and Panama Rock City west of Jamestown are the largest of all the rock cities and offer very dramatic and fascinating experiences not repeated elsewhere. Open to the public for a fee of several dollars, they are definitely worth the cost. For information, call (716) 372-7790 for Big Rock City and (716) 782-2845 for Panama Rock City.

The rock cities were formed by the gradual erosion of a layer of conglomerate rock that caps some hilltops in our region. Conglomerate, also called "pudding stone," is a pebble and cobble-studded rock that is very resistant to erosion and weathering. Over thousands of years, this rock developed cracks that widened, separating the cap rock into huge rectangular blocks of rock. Crevices formed between them, and the blocks very gradually slid down the hill slope due to gravity. As they slid, the crevices widened into "alleys" and "streets" and many boulders separated enough to end up scattered throughout the woods.

Remember to "thank" the Ice Age glaciers for giving us the opportunity to see these remarkable rock formations. All of the rock cities lie just south of where the Ice Age glaciers stopped 12,000 years ago before melting away. If the glaciers had continued south, they would have obliterated the rock cities, grinding some of the boulders into oblivion and scattering the rest over the land.

Directions:

From Buffalo, Ontario and Rochester, go to the NY Thruway (Rt. 90) west to Rt. 219 (Exit 55). Take 219 south to Springville (where it turns from a four-lane highway to a two-lane road) and continue southward along 219. Eight miles south of Ellicottville (or three miles south of Great Valley), watch carefully on your right for Hungry Hollow Road (ignore Mutton Hollow and Porter Hollow roads). If you start to enter the City of Salamanca, you have gone too far.

From Erie, Penn. and points west, take Rt. 17 east to Salamanca and turn north on Rt. 219. From Corning-Elmira direction, take Rt. 17 West. Rt. 219 joins with Rt. 17 west of Olean and then separates from it in Salamanca. At this junction, follow Rt. 219 north. If you are coming southward from Pennsylvania, take 219 through Bradford north to Rt. 17 west toward Salamanca, where you exit at Rt. 219 north. From where 219 north breaks off from Rt. 17, go several miles until you reach Hungry Hollow Rd.

Hungry Hollow Road starts off by travelling through a farming area, then makes a sharp left followed by a sharp right. It becomes a gravel road, enters the woods and climbs steeply up a hill. You'll pass the historic Civilian Conservation Corps Camp established during the Great Depression (1936 - 1941) to put people to work to reforest denuded lands. Near the hill crest, pass McCarthy Hill woods road (labelled "CCC Forest Road") to the right. The next left is Rock City Road, though you will see it labelled as "Truck Trail - Travel At Own Risk." You'll start noticing massive boulders in the woods, the outskirts of the "metropolitan area" of Little Rock City. You'll also pass picnic shelters. Take the road to its deadend loop.

When you reach the end of the loop, continue driving around it another 200 feet so that your car is facing out toward the way you came in. The Rock City is now to your right.

This is the time to orient yourself. You are at the top of a high hill ridge at an elevation of 2300 feet. The Rock City lies along the east side of the ridge, close to and paralleling the road which runs along the top of the ridge. Therefore, uphill will always take you back to the road.

A sign points toward the "Nature Trail," but do not follow the trail yet; this will be the suggested return trail. If you take this trail first, you are likely to miss "Broadway" and "Wall Street."

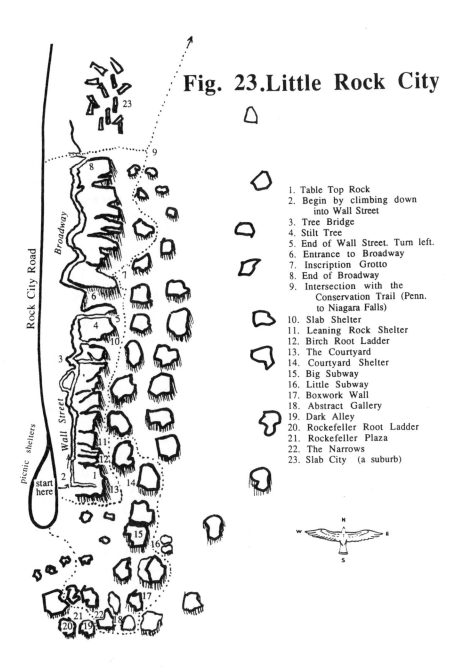

Fig. 23.Little Rock City

1. Table Top Rock
2. Begin by climbing down into Wall Street
3. Tree Bridge
4. Stilt Tree
5. End of Wall Street. Turn left.
6. Entrance to Broadway
7. Inscription Grotto
8. End of Broadway
9. Intersection with the Conservation Trail (Penn. to Niagara Falls)
10. Slab Shelter
11. Leaning Rock Shelter
12. Birch Root Ladder
13. The Courtyard
14. Courtyard Shelter
15. Big Subway
16. Little Subway
17. Boxwork Wall
18. Abstract Gallery
19. Dark Alley
20. Rockefeller Root Ladder
21. Rockefeller Plaza
22. The Narrows
23. Slab City   (a suburb)

Instead, head into the woods about 50 feet to the left of the sign and you will enter immediately onto a large flat rock called "Table Top Rock," which ends at a cliff.

You are now ready to explore this fascinating fantasy "city."

Just as you walk onto **Table Top Rock** from your car, notice a deep 4 to 5-foot wide crevice that extends away to your left, heading along the edge of the woods (not toward the cliff). This is **Wall Street** (at least a caveman's equivalent of New York City's Wall Street). Climb down into it and follow it as it winds between, squeezes through and goes over rock blocks. Check out every side passageway -- there will be surprises! Two alleyways lead out of it to the forest below the cliffs, while there are also little "ramps" that lead upward to the forest above. Check these out, too, but make sure to return to Wall Street, so you can walk it to its end. You will pass under a "tree bridge." Remember, in spring and during rainy periods, it can be quite muddy.

Finally, Wall Street will lead out to the right to the edge of the forest. Notice the **Stilt Tree**, a hemlock pressed into a crevice, standing on two tall root trunks. Continue skirting the cliff face on your left, and you will make a right-angle turn to the left. A short distance later, you will notice another wide street, **Broadway**. Enter this corridor and pick your way through it until it ultimately ends where it opens up into the forest.*

At this point, you will notice the pink blazes of the nature trail. If you head left, you will exit the Rock City and come to the road. But you will miss the other half of the fantasy land. So head right and follow the pink blazes. (Shortly after, you will meet up with a white and yellow-blazed trail to your left. This is the Conservation Trail, which connects Pennsylvania to Niagara Falls!)

The trail will weave between rock "buildings" and along ledges. As you continue walking on the nature trail, notice the huge, separated boulders in the woods to your left. These are the ones that have very gradually "crept" down the hill. Hundreds of these lie scattered about the hillside. If you visit any, always make sure you return to the pink trail to avoid getting disoriented.

Further down the trail, you will reach a cliff overhanging and forming an angular grotto about eight feet high and 15 feet deep

---

*Ahead of you, a short distance through the woods, is an optional side trip to a "suburb" called Slab City, named for the huge piles of rock slabs. If you go this, make sure you return to this same point so that you don't miss the sights along the return route.

(**Inscription Grotto**). Look carefully for the historic carvings by the early settlers that go back to the 1800s. How many can you decipher? The oldest we could find were "J.D. June 30, 1861", "Moall 1861", "Maggie Nash, Elmira, N.Y. Oct. 2, 1886", "B. Smith, L[ittle] Valley, N.Y. Aug. 29, '94" (that's _18_94!). Can you find any older ones? **Do not damage them or try to carve any new ones! They've survived this long and now they're a historic treasure.**

After you round the corner of the grotto rock, you will see the entrance to Broadway again. A short distance later, you'll make another right angle around another "building" and you'll notice the exit to Wall Street again. Just after that, look along the ledge for the **Slab Shelter**, located six feet up and reached by a series of ledge steps. A little further, you will enter **The Courtyard**. A short distance off the pink trail are **Leaning Rocks Shelter** and the **Birch Root Ladder**. Right after these, look carefully on you right for the **Courtyard Shelter** which has a tiny peephole of light way inside at its dark end. See if you can find it!

Only a few "buildings" later, look for the **Big Subway** on the right, and then the **Little Subway** on the left. These are cave-like tunnels through the boulders. Next along the trail are the **Abstract Galleries**, two rock walls with "boxwork," curious erosion patterns that look like contorted ridges, hollows and pockmarks caused by dissolving of the cement that holds the sand grains together. Two long and narrow passageways, **Dark Alley** and **The Narrows**, can be found up the trail. Unlike human cities, however, you won't find any criminals hiding in their shadows! Finally, you enter **Rockefeller Plaza**, a whimsical reminder of the famous landmark in Manhattan. Notice its root ladder up the rock face.

The pink trail will leave this bizarre Stone Age courtyard and soon will return you to your car.

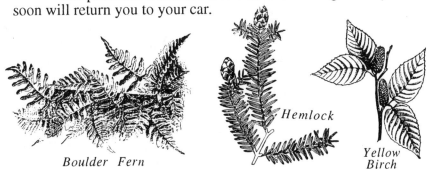

Boulder Fern

Hemlock

Yellow Birch

PAPA, MAMA AND BABY BEAR CAVES

Scenic woodland walk to a "rock city" jumble of giant boulders and three fun caves.

Distance: This description covers only the 1/2-mile round trip to Bear Caves rock city. It is the beginning section of the Mt. Seneca Trail. If you want to continue on the rest of this 3-mile long trail, it loops up and over Mt. Seneca, a moderately strenuous climb of 800 feet.

Level of Difficulty: The trail to the caves is easy. Crawling through the caves varies from moderate to difficult because of the climbing, twisting, ducking and uneven footing. Some larger adults may be excluded because of their size.

Notable Features:

Bear Caves: A small "rock city" in Allegany State Park. It is one of 29 rock cities in the area, only nine of which accessible to the public. It is a line of massive, jumbled rectangular boulders along the edge of a cliff. (See the Little Rock City description for a full description of what these unique rock cities are and how they formed.) Bear Caves may be one of the smaller rock cities, but it has the deepest caves of all the rock cities. While they were once real bear dens long ago, no self-respecting bear uses these popular (with humans) shelters anymore. **All four Bear Caves are safe for children to enter and explore with adult supervision.**

Papa Bear Cave: A 120-foot deep cave that turns at right angles through tall but narrow "halls." Halfway in you can encounter several-inch deep water, so bring boots. Papa Bear (and humans with beer bellies or big frames) would have a difficult time getting through these halls.

Mama Bear Cave: A 30-foot oblong room entered from a hole at the top of the cliff. The ceiling is as high as 20 feet and has a little skylight hole in it. A window in the rock lies at the bottom end, allowing the explorer to peer out into the forest or exit from the bottom. Similarly, the lower cave

Massive boulders of Bear Caves Rock City

entrance can be entered from the cliff-bottom path.

Baby Bear Cave. A 7 by 4-foot long rectangular room with a unique slit-like window at its back end. If there are other people exploring near this spot, you can see them or mischievously call to them without their being able to figure out where you are. (I think Goldilocks' Baby Bear would do something like that!)

Bear Grotto: A 15 foot-deep rock shelter with a short passageway into the back that connects a little rectangular, cliff-lined "courtyard" with the bottom of the rock city cliff. From the bottom approach, the secret courtyard is hidden behind boulders; from the above approach, you can peer into it.

Equipment needed: Take along a flashlight, boots, a child-like curiosity and a sense of adventure.

Use caution when climbing on the rocks. Avoid hitting your head while caving.

Directions:

From Buffalo, take NY Thruway west to Rt. 219. Take 219 south all the way to Allegany State Park, 90 minutes drive from Buffalo. From Rochester, take Rt. 390 south to Rt. 17, which you take west directly to the park. From points further east, take the NY Thruway (Rt. 90) to Rt. 390, or Rt. 17 west. From Erie, Pennsylvania and points west, take Rt. 17 east. From the south, take Rt. 219 north to Rt. 17 west, or Rt. 62 to Rt. 17 east. Once you are close to Allegany State Park, signs will point you to it.

Once in the park, go to park headquarters at Red House Lake and take State Park (ASP) Road #1 south until it ends at ASP #3 at south end of the park. Turn left on ASP #3 and drive exactly 1.6 miles, looking for trailhead parking for Bear Caves-Mt. Seneca Trail #2. The parking lot is across the street from the trailhead.

From the beginning of the trail, it is only 1/4 mile to Bear Caves. The trail starts to climb immediately and passes **Balanced Rock** on the left. You will know you have reached Bear Caves Rock City when a large collection of giant square boulders appears directly in front of you. Here is where the trail forks. The right fork heads straight up the cliff, the left route follows along the bottom of

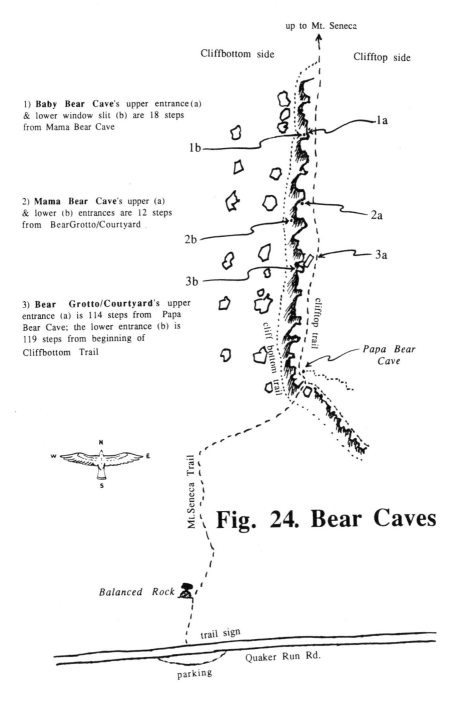

up to Mt. Seneca

Cliffbottom side   Clifftop side

1) **Baby Bear Cave**'s upper entrance (a)
& lower window slit (b) are 18 steps
from Mama Bear Cave

1a

1b

2) **Mama Bear Cave**'s upper (a)
& lower (b) entrances are 12 steps
from BearGrotto/Courtyard

2a

2b

3a

3b

3) **Bear Grotto/Courtyard**'s upper
entrance (a) is 114 steps from Papa
Bear Cave; the lower entrance (b) is
119 steps from beginning of
Cliffbottom Trail

clifftop trail

cliff bottom trail

Papa Bear Cave

N
W   E
S

Mt. Seneca Trail

Fig. 24. Bear Caves

Balanced Rock

trail sign

Quaker Run Rd.

parking

the line of cliffs. Take the the one that climbs up steeply. *As soon as you reach the top of the ledge*, look for **Papa Bear Cave** entrance in front of you to your right, only five feet from the trail and 12 feet in from the edge of the cliff. The entrance is two to three feet high and 1.5 feet wide, but it enlarges immediately to the height of an adult. See if you can reach its back end, 120 feet in.

To locate the back entrance of **Bear Grotto**, start walking from Papa Bear Cave's opening and count your steps as you walk the trail along the top of the ledges. Roughly 114 (adult) steps away, you will notice the box-like Bear Courtyard below you to your left. Climb down into it to its back end and you will find the hidden entrance into Baby Bear Grotto.

To locate **Mama Bear Cave**, walk 12 to 15 steps further than Bear Courtyard (126 from Papa Bear Cave). Step down onto the lower rock shelf, walk to the outer edge of the cliff and look for a vertical hole in a crevice. This is the entrance. It may look unlikely, but slender adults and kids can climb down it with flashlights; with a bit of twisting, you will emerge into the cave room. Trust me!

Once inside Mama Bear Cave, look for the hole in the ceiling and the lower entrance at the back end. While you can exit from here, the directions to the next cave require you to start from the top entrance of this cave.

To locate **Baby Bear Cave**, walk roughly 18 more steps (144 from Papa Bear Cave) further from the upper opening of Mama Bear Cave. Look for a vertical opening and drop down into a rectangular room, seven feet long and 4 feet wide. At its rear end is a narrow window where you can look out into the forest.

If you want to know how to locate the cave entrances from the trail that follows the *bottom* of the ledges, start at the fork where the two trails separate. Bear Grotto will be roughly 119 steps ahead; Mama Bear Cave's lower entrance (4 feet high, 18 inches wide) will be 12 steps further; and Baby Bear's slit-like window will be 18 steps further than that. (Papa Bear Cave has no entrance from the bottom.)

Note: If you choose to take the Mt. Seneca Trail past Bear Caves, you will climb Mt. Seneca and then descend to ASP #3 at the west entrance of the trail. It is a half-mile walk along the road back to the east end of the trail.

JAKES ROCKS JAUNT

Explore the rugged rock formations, crevice caves and impressive cliffs of Jakes Rocks and enjoy the breathtaking panoramas over the Allegheny Hills and Allegheny Reservoir.

Distance: 1.5 miles

Difficulty: Moderate to strenuous.

Notable Features:

Allegheny National Forest: A half-million acre National Forest bordering New York State and Allegany State Park. While most of it is heavily logged-over lands and oil and gas drilling rigs, it also has many beautiful sights scattered throughout it. These include Tionesta Creek Virgin Forest, Hearts Content Virgin Forest, Hickory Creek Wilderness Area, Minister Creek Scenic Area and Allegheny Front National Recreation Area. The author chose to select just this one attraction since it is the closest to New York State. When you visit the Forest, pick up maps at a ranger station so you can see these other outstanding areas.

Jakes Rocks: A long, jagged cliff overlooking the Allegheny Reservoir. It provides several outstanding panoramas of the Allegheny Hills and plateaus. A trail descends to its base and weaves under jutting overhangs, massive boulder jumbles, odd rock shapes and narrow caves (one named Indian Cave). Jakes Rocks is really another of the Rock Cities that are so extensive in New York's Southern Tier (see the description of Rock Cities under Little Rock City).

Directions:

From Buffalo, Rochester and Ontario, take NY Thruway (Rt. 90) west and exit onto Rt. 219. Take Rt. 219 south until the highway portion turns into a two-lane road at Springville. Continue on Rt. 219 into Salamanca, where you follow signs to Rt. 17 east. From New York's Southern Tier and the City of Erie, Pa., take Rt. 17 toward Salamanca.

Leave Rt. 17 at its exit for Rt. 219 *South*, located between Salamanca and Olean. Take Rt. 219 south into Pennsylvania through the city of Bradford. Past Bradford, look for Rt. 770 into

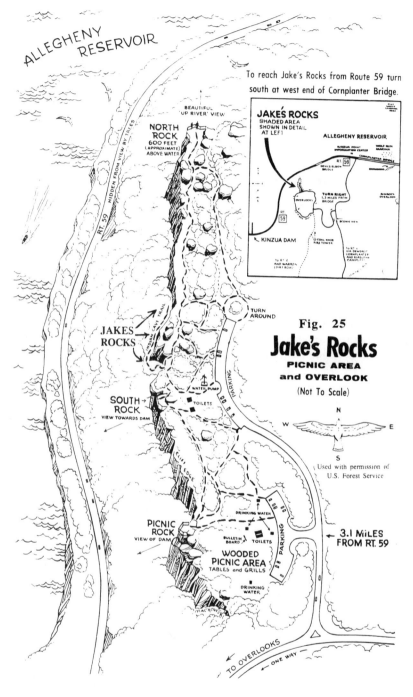

ALLEGHENY RESERVOIR

To reach Jake's Rocks from Route 59 turn
south at west end of Cornplanter Bridge.

JAKE'S ROCKS
SHADED AREA
SHOWN IN DETAIL
AT LEFT

ALLEGHENY RESERVOIR

BEAUTIFUL
'UP RIVER' VIEW

NORTH
ROCK
600 FEET
(APPROXIMATE)
ABOVE WATER

TURN RIGHT
1.3 MILES FROM
BRIDGE

KINZUA DAM

JAKES
ROCKS

TURN
AROUND

WATER PUMP

TOILETS

SOUTH
ROCK
VIEW TOWARDS DAM

Fig. 25

Jake's Rocks
PICNIC AREA
and OVERLOOK
(Not To Scale)

N
W   E
S

(Used with permission of
U.S. Forest Service)

DRINKING WATER

PICNIC
ROCK
VIEW OF DAM

BULLETIN
BOARD   TOILETS

**WOODED
PICNIC AREA**
TABLES and GRILLS

← 3.1 MILES
FROM RT. 59

DRINKING
WATER

TO OVERLOOKS   ONE WAY

the National Forest. It ends at Rt. 59. Make a right (west) on Rt. 59. Take it across the Forest until you reach Allegheny Reservoir.

Cross Cornplanter Bridge over the Reservoir. **Immediately upon reaching the other side, turn left onto a road (Road 262).** If you come to the Kinzua Point Information Center, you've passed it. Once on Rt. 262, drive 1.3 miles and make a right onto a small road. Drive 1.8 miles, turning onto the first paved road on the right. Drive to the last parking area and park.

Take one of the trails to South Rock Overlook Point (see trail map). Just to the right of it (when facing toward the ledge) is the trail that descends to the bottom of the cliff. Follow it to its end, making sure to explore every nook and cranny.

When you're done with your exploration, turn back the same way came and climb to the cliff top. Walk along the cliff edge both ways to see the different views from North Rock and Picnic Rock Overlooks. You can picnic here.

Under the cliffs and boulders of Jakes Rocks

THE WORLD'S MOST PERFECT PLACE
FOR SKIPPING ROCKS -- CANADAWAY CREEK

A walk to one of the last wild, undeveloped stretches of Lake Erie coast in New York State, and a beach which qualifies as the most perfect place for skipping rocks.

Distance: 1/2 mile round trip

Level of Difficulty: Easy

Notable Features:

Canadaway Creek Nature Sanctuary: A 33-acre nature preserve owned by The Nature Conservancy located at the mouth of Canadaway Creek where it empties into Lake Erie. While relatively small, the sanctuary provides public access to one of the last wild shores of New York's Lake Erie's coast. The lonely, rocky beach extends a third of a mile to where it ends at a cliffy bluff. It narrows to only a several foot-wide gravel spit which almost cuts off Canadaway Creek. The sanctuary is recognized as an outstanding place to see birds because it is a major stopover point for migrating birds in spring and fall and it offers protected river stretches for waterfowl. More than 160 birds have been sighted, including whistling swan, Caspian tern, wood duck, black crowned night heron and 22 species of warblers.

In addition, the sanctuary also offers a rock-skipping paradise for kids and kids-at-heart. One does not have to search for skipping rocks here! The beach is completely composed of flat and razor-thin shale rocks of every size. Even more, kids have choices of *two* types of water to cast their stones across. You can skip stones into Lake Erie's waves (bet ya' can't skip it all the way to Canada!). Or by just turning around on the extremely narrow peninsula, you can skip it across the creek's flat waters behind you. My record for skipping was 11 bounces before the "skipper" rock disappeared into the water.

The Nature Conservancy. A national non-profit organization that has accomplished one of the most amazing feats of any organization -- it is the world's largest owner of private nature preserves. The TNC and its 600,000 members have acquired 1300 preserves comprising 6.4 million acres, the size of the state of Maryland. Properties are purchased based on their ecological value

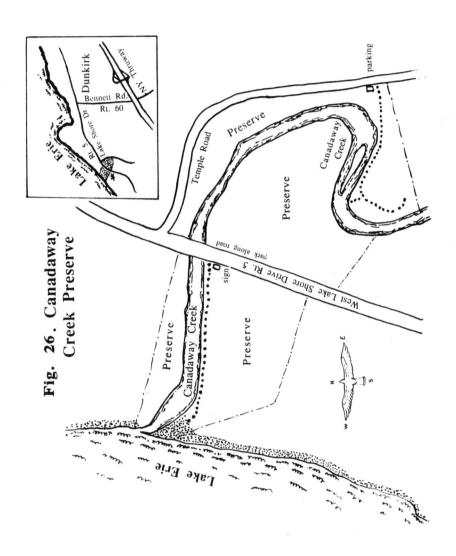

Fig. 26. Canadaway Creek Preserve

such as endangered species, old growth forests or critical habitat. The Western NY chapter owns ten preserves totalling more than 1200 acres, including Canadaway Creek. If you wish to learn more about this remarkable tax-deductible group, contact the TNC at 1815 N. Lynn Street, Arlington, Va. 22209, (703) 841-5300 or the Western NY office at 315 Alexander St., Suite 301, Rochester, NY 14604, (716) 546-8030.

Directions:

From Ontario, take Queen Elizabeth Way to Buffalo, cross at the Peace Bridge, and take Rt. 190 south to NY Thruway (Rt. 90) west. From Buffalo, Rochester or points east, take the NY Thruway (Rt. 90) west to Exit 59 - Dunkirk-Rt.60. From Salamanca, Olean and points east, take Rt. 17 west to Exit 12 and head north on Rt. 60 into Dunkirk.

Once on Rt. 60 north (Bennett Road) in Dunkirk, take it to Lake Shore Drive (Rt. 5). Turn left and proceed about 2.5 miles to the sanctuary at the outskirts of town. It is located where the road crosses the creek; a large wooden sign identifies the preserve. You may park along Rt. 5. The trail begins at the bridge. Parking is also located 1/8 mile up Temple Road off Rt. 5, on the right. This second trail leads through bird-filled thickets to secluded stretches of meandering river for a very different setting. Bring mosquito protection in the summer!

Skippin' a rock into Lake Erie at Canadaway Creek

Index

Index